Windows 11
SENIORS GUIDE

THE MOST UPDATED CRASH COURSE FOR THE NON-TECH-SAVVY TO MASTER ALL THE FUNCTIONS OF WINDOWS 11

Jay Thorne

TABLE OF CONTENTS

INTRODUCTION

The new Windows 11 has a lot to offer, but it's possible that you're not aware of all of the new features and functions it brings. Many people are perplexed when Microsoft releases new versions of Windows. What is the difference between the old and new versions?

In this book, we'll look at all of Windows 11's most overlooked features as well as the significantly redesigned interface for seniors.

Microsoft released Windows 10 as a service in two installments, the first being the Windows 10 Anniversary Update and the second being the Windows 10 Creators Update.

One of the most noticeable changes in the Creator's Update was the addition of the Cortana digital assistant. While Windows 10 included built-in Cortana features, the Creators Update enhanced those features to improve the user experience.

Cortana can be accessed via a variety of methods, including the "Hey Cortana" hotkey, taskbar hotkey buttons, and the Cortana screen. Cortana can also be accessed via the notification panel on the taskbar and the new Cortana screen to search for information, get weather updates, and open programs.

On the new screen, you can quickly search your contact list, the web, or your most recent emails. The latest version of Windows (11) also lets you use Cortana to search your device's local files and perform other tasks.

Cortana is now integrated into the Windows desktop with Windows 11. This means that if you ask Cortana a question while on your desktop, Windows will go to work, find the answer, and present it to you.

That's pretty cool, isn't it? However, there are numerous other cool features in Windows 11 that you are not aware of. Let's get started.

CHAPTER 1

A BRIEF HISTORY OF WINDOWS

Let's take a quick look at how the Windows operating system has evolved and changed so you can fully appreciate the features available in the latest version.

Windows 1 was Microsoft's first release, and it featured a very simple graphical user interface in which a mouse could control a cursor on the screen. A few years later, Windows 2 arrived, introducing the ability to use 16-color graphic displays. These displays generated various information windows, which could be minimized and maximized. Windows 2 also included the first versions of the office programs Microsoft Word and Microsoft Excel.

Windows 3 was the first to be distributed on a CD-ROM. It saw the release of various managers that assisted users in performing various tasks rather than relying on command-line prompts or lines of code. Some of these managers, such as the File Manager, Control Panel, Print Manager, and Program Manager, are still used in modern versions. Windows 3 added 256 colors to the interface, allowing it to be modernized and customized, as well as networking features that allowed connections to be established between multiple computers.

Windows 95 is one of the first versions of the operating system to resemble modern versions, with the Taskbar spanning the bottom of the screen and the Start Menu in the left-hand corner. Windows 95 included dial-up internet access and the first version of the Internet Explorer browser. It also included multimedia features like automatic configuration of various pieces of multimedia hardware, applications for working with video, sound, graphics, and images, and video support with higher frame rates and faster processing speeds.

The demand for resources increased as the versions were updated. Windows 98, which was released in 1998, required more memory and storage space than previous versions, and many computers did not come standard with this hardware, necessitating the user's purchase of the necessary upgrades. However, this was a small price to pay for the added features and functionality. Windows 98 supported not only CD-ROMs, but also DVDs and USB flash drives. Additional features for managing background processes, such as an update manager, internet sharing manager, and disk cleanup, have been added.

Windows 2000 was released with the hope that it would be adopted for a variety of business purposes, as it provided unique business solutions such as file encryption to keep data safe and secure, as well as server capabilities.

Windows XP was by far Microsoft's most successful product, selling over 17 million licensed copies in the two months following its release (Microsoft, 2002). In contrast to Windows 2000, which was marketed to business users, Windows XP was crafted and designed for the average home user. It had a new look with transparent windows, drop shadows, and customizable visual styles. The Start menu was modified and updated to include a two-column layout displaying all installed applications as well as frequently used programs and documents. This version also included a firewall to help protect the computer from internet traffic and the ability to burn CDs.

Windows Vista was one of Microsoft's least successful versions, struggling to compete with Windows XP's massive success. It improved some aspects of graphics display and memory management, but it required much more hardware, making it inefficient and prone to bugs. Many programs compatible with Windows XP would no longer be supported by Windows Vista, and there were other general changes to the interface's appearance that consumers disliked.

Windows 7 was released in 2009 and was designed specifically to meet the needs of wireless devices such as laptop computers. It included touch, speech, and handwriting recognition, making it easier to use for people with disabilities, and it supported a wider range of file formats. The taskbar was upgraded and decluttered once more, making it run more efficiently and providing the user with a more streamlined experience. The file manager was improved and optimized, and the system requirements were not significantly higher than in previous versions. Many users skipped Windows Vista entirely and went straight from Windows XP to Windows 7.

Windows 8 was a significant risk because Microsoft attempted to capitalize on the touch screens provided by many mobile devices, including laptops, tablets, and smartphones. This version did not fare well and was short-lived, but it saw changes such as a completely revamped interface with a tile-style start menu and the removal of the start button entirely. Although this version had faster startup times, many users who had grown accustomed to the previous layout and interfaces found it difficult to adjust to such drastic changes.

Windows 10 (yes, there was no version 9) saw a return to the more traditional desktop with the removal of the tile interface. It supports universal apps that work across multiple devices, such as Photos, Videos, Music, Mail, Calendar, and Messaging. Touch-based and mouse-based interfaces, a new internet browser called Microsoft Edge, a redesigned Start menu, and Cortana integration are among the other features. Cortana is a voice-controlled digital assistant that can assist in problem solving and task completion without the use of a mouse or keyboard.

What exactly is Windows 11?

Windows 11 is the most recent version of Microsoft's operating system. An operating system manages all software and hardware on your computer, laptop, or tablet, ensuring that all files, programs, and processes have efficient and adequate access to the hard drives, processing units, memory, and storage.

Over the years, various versions of Windows have been released. Windows 1 was released in 1985, and since then, it has evolved into more modern versions such as Windows 95, Windows XP, Windows 7, Windows 8, Windows 10, and the most recent version, which we will discuss in this book. Each version has seen updates and changes to how the operating system looks and feels, as well as more technical changes that run in the background to improve your computer experience.

Other operating systems for computers include Linux, Ubuntu, Android, ChromeOS, and macOS. Each of these operating systems is tailored to the specific requirements of different users. Some are better at office tasks like writing documents and emails, while others are better at writing code and developing software. Operating systems are also designed for different types of devices; for example, smartphones use Android or IOS, which are designed for mobile devices and are best suited for running small apps, whereas computers require more comprehensive operating systems that include a variety of hardware and software.

Windows 11, like other operating systems, provides a graphical user interface. This is a method of communicating with your computer system, mouse, or touchscreen by clicking on various symbols or icons. Character user interfaces were used before graphical user interfaces became the norm. To carry out various tasks and functions in a character user interface or command-line interface, you would need to write specific lines of code or commands.

CHAPTER 2

COMPARISON BETWEEN WINDOWS 10 AND 11

Differences Between Windows 10 And Windows 11

Windows 11 includes a number of new features that help users manage multiple tasks with multiple windows and work with multiple monitors.

The updates' quality has also improved. Updates are now up to 40% smaller in size, and Windows will install them in the background. In addition, unlike Windows 10, Windows 11 will only receive one major upgrade per year, rather than the two received by Windows 10.

Microsoft has updated the taskbar with a widgets pane and Microsoft Teams integration for simple talking and calling.

The Microsoft Store in Windows 11 has significantly improved: it now contains any Windows app desired. Android apps are now available and can be downloaded from the Google Play Store.

There are several PC gaming modifications. Auto HDR and DirectStorage have made their way from the Xbox Series X to the PC, enhancing graphics in classic games and reducing latency in modern games on powerful PCs.

Difference in Specs

	Windows 11	Windows 10
Processor	1GHz or faster with 2+ cores on a 64-bit processor/SoC	1GHz or faster processor/SoC
RAM:	4GB	1GB for 32-bit / 2GB for 64-bit
Storage	64GB or more	16GB for 32-bit / 20GB for 64-bit
System firmware:	UEFI, Secure Boot capable	N/A
TPM:	Trusted Platform Module (TPM) version 2.0	N/A
Graphics card:	DirectX 12 or later with WDDM 2.0 driver	DirectX 9 or later with WDDM 1.0 driver
Display:	720p display that is greater than 9-inch diagonally, 8 bits per colour channel	800 x 600 display
Internet access required?	Yes	No

CHAPTER 3

KEYBOARD FUNCTION AND HOW TO SETUP MOUSE AND KEYBOARD

Touch Keyboard

For those that have a touch screen, one of the great features in Windows 11 is touch keyboard. This Windows update automatically improves the touch targets of spacing on the Taskbar and also positions a touch keyboard toggle in the System Tray.

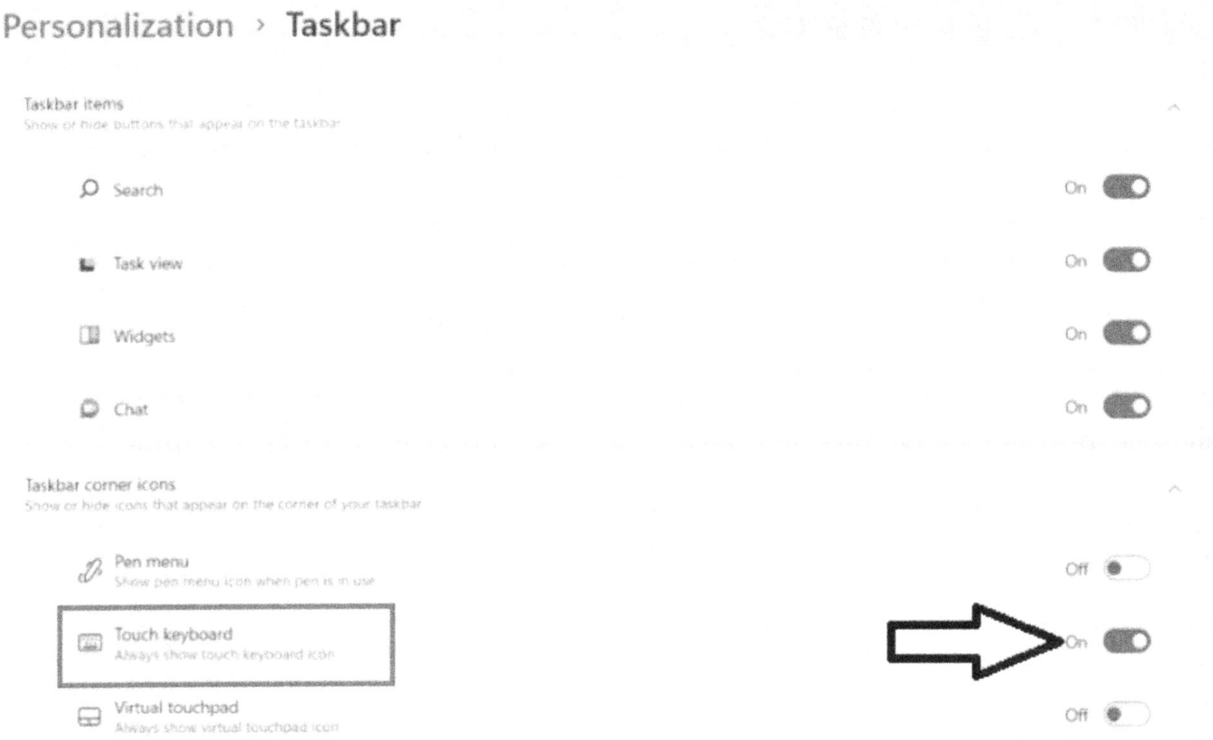

To easily enable touch keyboard, right click on the Taskbar and then select **Taskbar settings.** Under **Taskbar** within the **Personalization setting**, go to the option Touch keyboard and toggle it **On**. This will in turn add the touch keyboard toggle to the right side of the Taskbar. Now when you are using a touch screen, click the keyboard toggle to launch the touch keyboard.

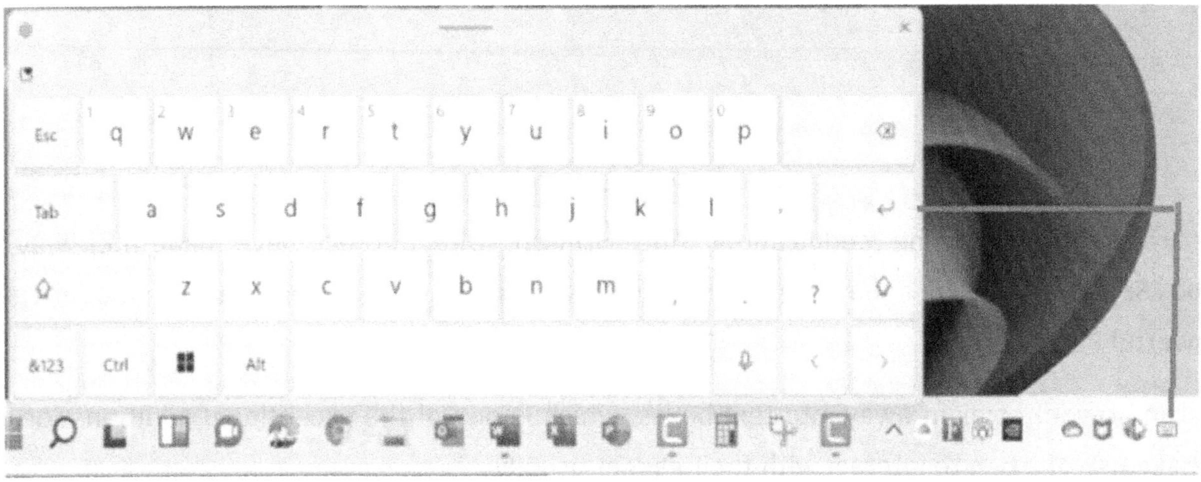

This new keyboard comes with subtle animations, perfect pleasurable sounds alongside error-free spelling correction based on SwiftKey operating in the background.

Windows 11 includes a number of new features that help users manage multiple tasks with multiple windows and work with multiple monitors.

The updates' quality has also improved. Updates are now up to 40% smaller in size, and Windows will install them in the background. In addition, unlike Windows 10, Windows 11 will only receive one major upgrade per year, rather than the two received by Windows 10.

Microsoft has updated the taskbar with a widgets pane and Microsoft Teams integration for simple talking and calling.

The Microsoft Store in Windows 11 has significantly improved: it now contains any Windows app desired. Android apps are now available and can be downloaded from the Google Play Store.

There are several PC gaming modifications. Auto HDR and DirectStorage have made their way from the Xbox Series X to the PC, enhancing graphics in classic games and reducing latency in modern games on powerful PCs.

Users can now ink straight away into text boxes, which is one of the exceptional additions for those who make use of a pen to interact with their gadget usually.

With Windows 11, users don't need to jump between tapping and inking on the display to type text into a search field, as the handwriting interface will automatically come up for them to engage with when tapping on a text field with a pen.

Choosing New Mouse Pointer And Touch

With Windows 11 Operating System, you can choose new pointer different from the one you are using on your computer by default. Some people like making their computers work in a fashionable way. As a result of that, they choose new mouse pointer design. Some may like bolder pointer while some others like the one that is designed as human palm. Whichever is your favorite, I will guide you on how you can change the default mouse pointer of your computer running Windows 11 Operating System.

To start with the change, click the **Search icon** pinned at the taskbar of your computer. In the search space, type "mouse pointer and touch". Some search results will be displayed. From the search results, click **Mouse pointer and touch** which is indicated in the photo below

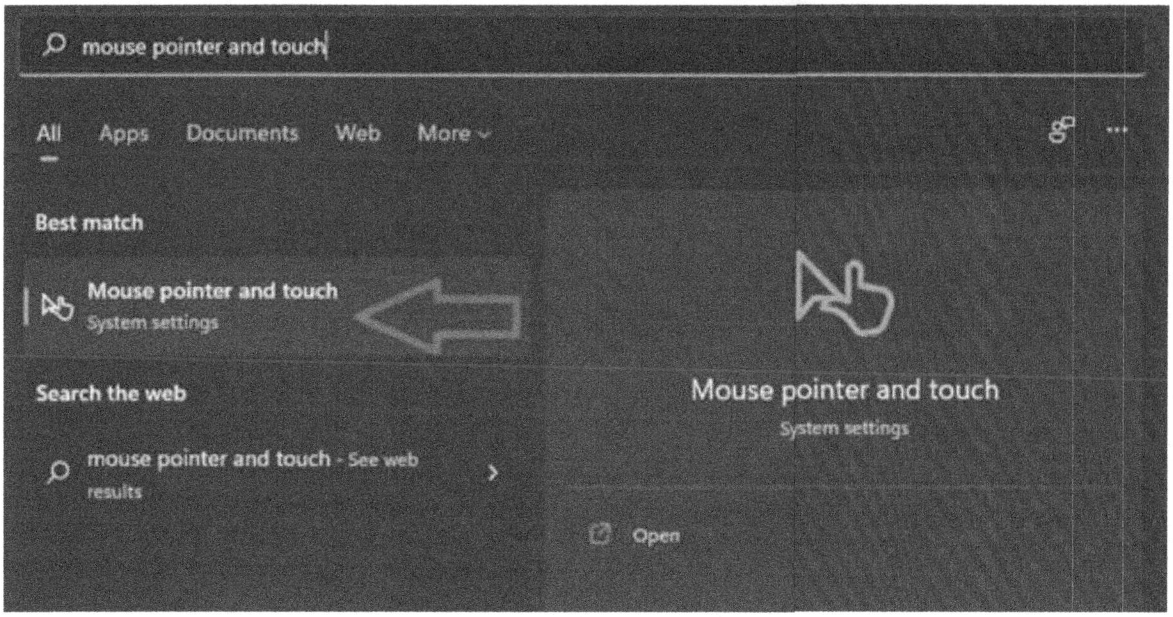

On clicking the **Mouse pointer and touch**, a new page will open where you are to select new pointer of your choice, and you can increase the size of pointer from the page as well. The photo below is the screenshot of the page.

Under the Mouse pointer style heading, you can select any new pointer from the above image. Simply click the pointer style of your choice, and the change will be applied immediately. There are four pointer styles available: white, black, inverted, and custom. Make your selection with a single click.

You can, additionally, change the size of any pointer style you're using. To increase the size of your mouse, drag the size to the right-hand side of the Size heading. The size decreases as you move to the left. You will notice a gradual change as you go through the process.

On the Mouse pointer and touch page, you can also change the touch indicator. The feature is disabled by default in the Touch indicator settings. When you turn it on, your pointer appears as a circle on your computer's screen when you touch it somewhere. To enable touch indicator on your computer running Windows 11, simply turn it on. The section is highlighted in the above image. You may need to restart your computer for the change to take effect completely.

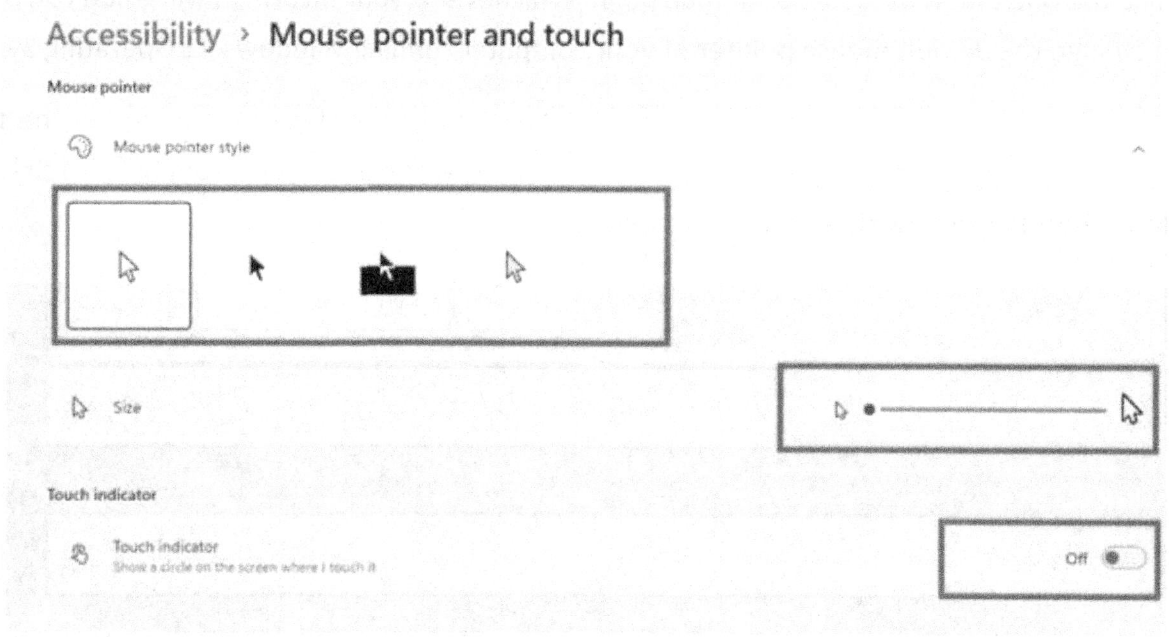

CHAPTER 4

HOW TO SETUP WINDOWS 11 FOR THE FIRST TIME

It is necessary to explain how to install this valuable software on your computer. It is critical because no computer can function without an operating system. Do you see the significance of an operating system now?

Also, before attempting to install Windows 11 on your computer, there are some basic requirements that your computer must meet. They are called basic because they are fundamental. We can skip the other requirements because we can jump them, and I'll show you how under a specific subheading.

Before installing the Windows 11 Operating System on your computer, the following basic requirements must be met: (1) Your computer must have a minimum of 4GB RAM, (2) a minimum disc space of 64GB, (3) your computer's processor must be 1GigaHertz or faster with 2 or more cores, (4) your computer must have a 720P display, (5) your computer must be running Windows 10 before the upgrade, and (6) your computer must be able to connect to the internet.

Returning to the main point of this subheading. These are the methods for installing Windows11 OS (Operating System) on your computer. The methods are as follows:

Upgrade via your PC's Update and Security Settings

Upgrade via Microsoft's website

Update and Security Upgrade to Windows 11

Many Windows computer users believe that upgrading your PC running Windows 10 to Windows 11 via the Update and Security settings is the quickest option. Either of the two methods I listed is appropriate for you. What matters is that your computer system is upgraded to the most recent operating system at the end.

These are the steps you must take to upgrade your personal computer to Windows 11 Operating System via the Update and Security of your computer:

Connect your computer to the internet. You can connect to the internet via Wi-Fi or through a data subscription. What is required is that your computer be connected to active internet data.

On your computer keyboard, press the Start button. Alternatively, you can use your computer's Start menu.

*The Please note that the abbreviation **OS** stands for **Operating System***

- The next step you need to take is click the **Settings icon** which is indicated in the photo below.

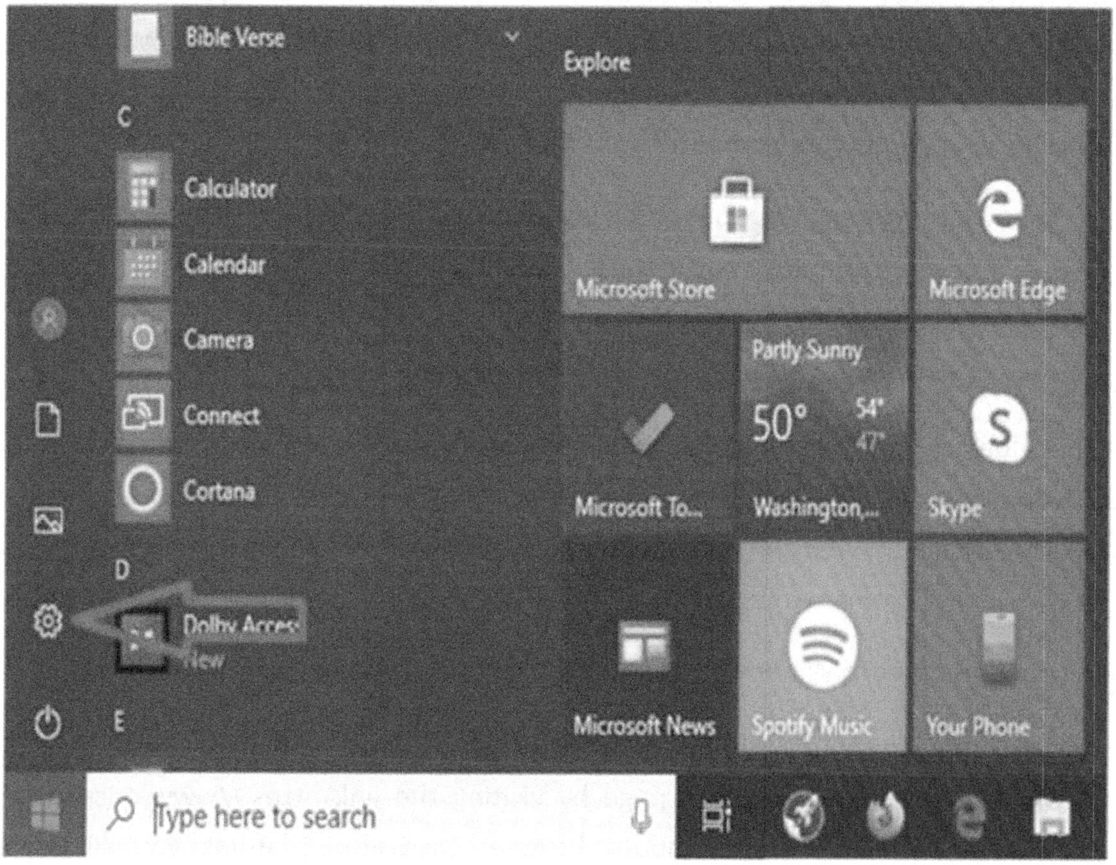

- As you select the Settings icon, you will see all the sub settings options available in your computer. On seeing them, click the **Update & Security** option, which I indicate in the photo below.

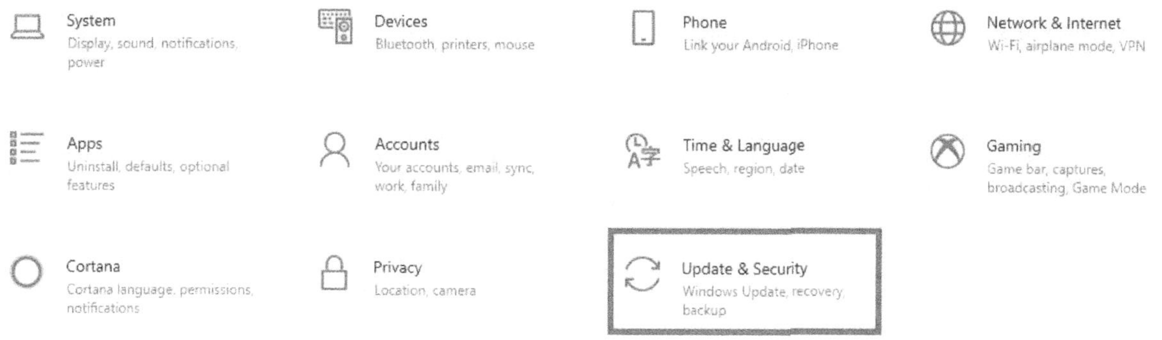

A new window will open on your computer as you complete the preceding step. This is the location where you can upgrade your Windows 10 computer to the Windows 11 operating system. If you see text that says "Update to Windows 11 is ready - and it's free!" you are almost done switching from Windows 10 to Windows 11.

Click on the Download and install button. That button is located beneath the Windows update.

As you complete this final step, the software will begin to download on your computer. When the downloading is complete, the installation process begins. Follow the prompts, and Windows 11 will be installed on your computer. Agree if the Windows 11 program asks if you want the downloaded program to make changes to your computer.

Please be patient while Windows 11 OS is being installed on your computer. The installation may take several minutes, and your computer may restart several times before it is finished.

Upgrading to Windows 11 through the Microsoft Website

If the just concluded approach I taught you on how to upgrade your computer running Windows 10 to Windows 11 does not work or you do not want to use that approach, another way you can do the upgrade is via the Microsoft website. Know that upgrade to Windows 11 Operating System is free, and therefore it will not cost you anything.

To upgrade your computer to Windows 11, these are the steps you need to take:

- Get your computer connected to the internet.
- Visit Microsoft Windows upgrade page by visiting the link https://www.microsoft.com/en-us/software-download in your computer browser. On visiting that link, you will be landed on the supported Microsoft Windows page, which is what I have displayed in the photo below.

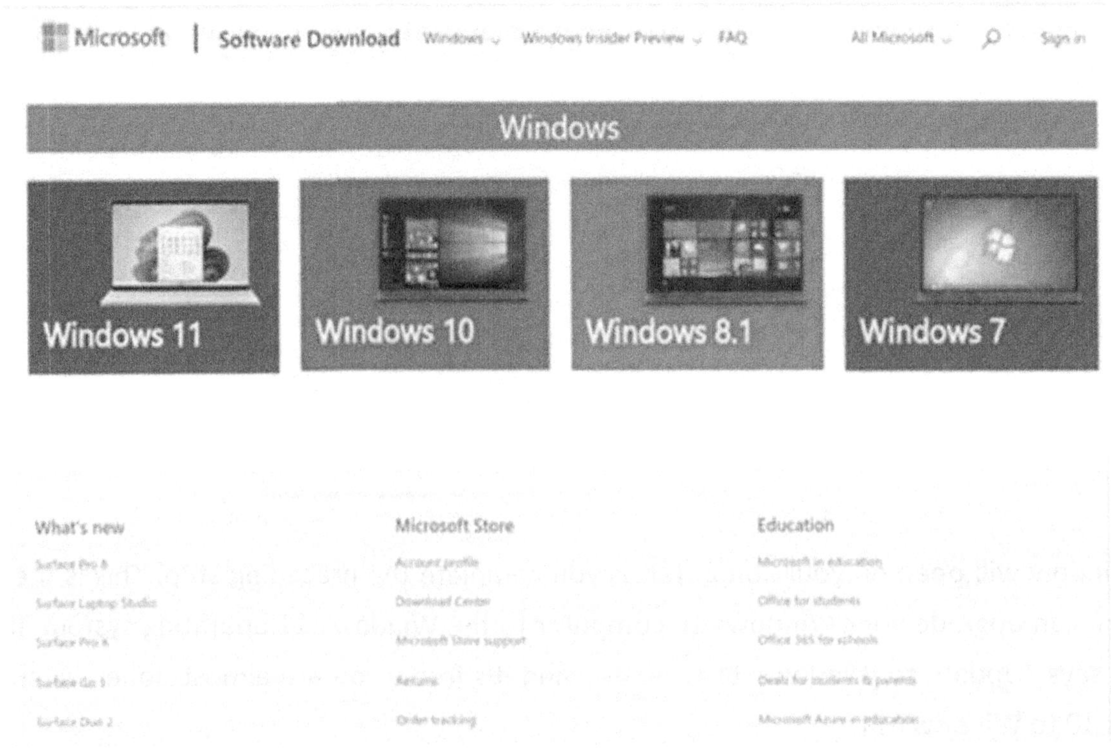

As you can see above, all Windows versions still supported by Microsoft Windows computers are on the page. They are Windows 7, Windows 8.1, Windows 10 and the latest, Windows 11. Our interest is on Windows 11, so we move.

- From the list of Windows, click **Windows 11** which is our interest. On taking that step, you will be taken to Windows 11 download page which is what I have in the screenshot below.

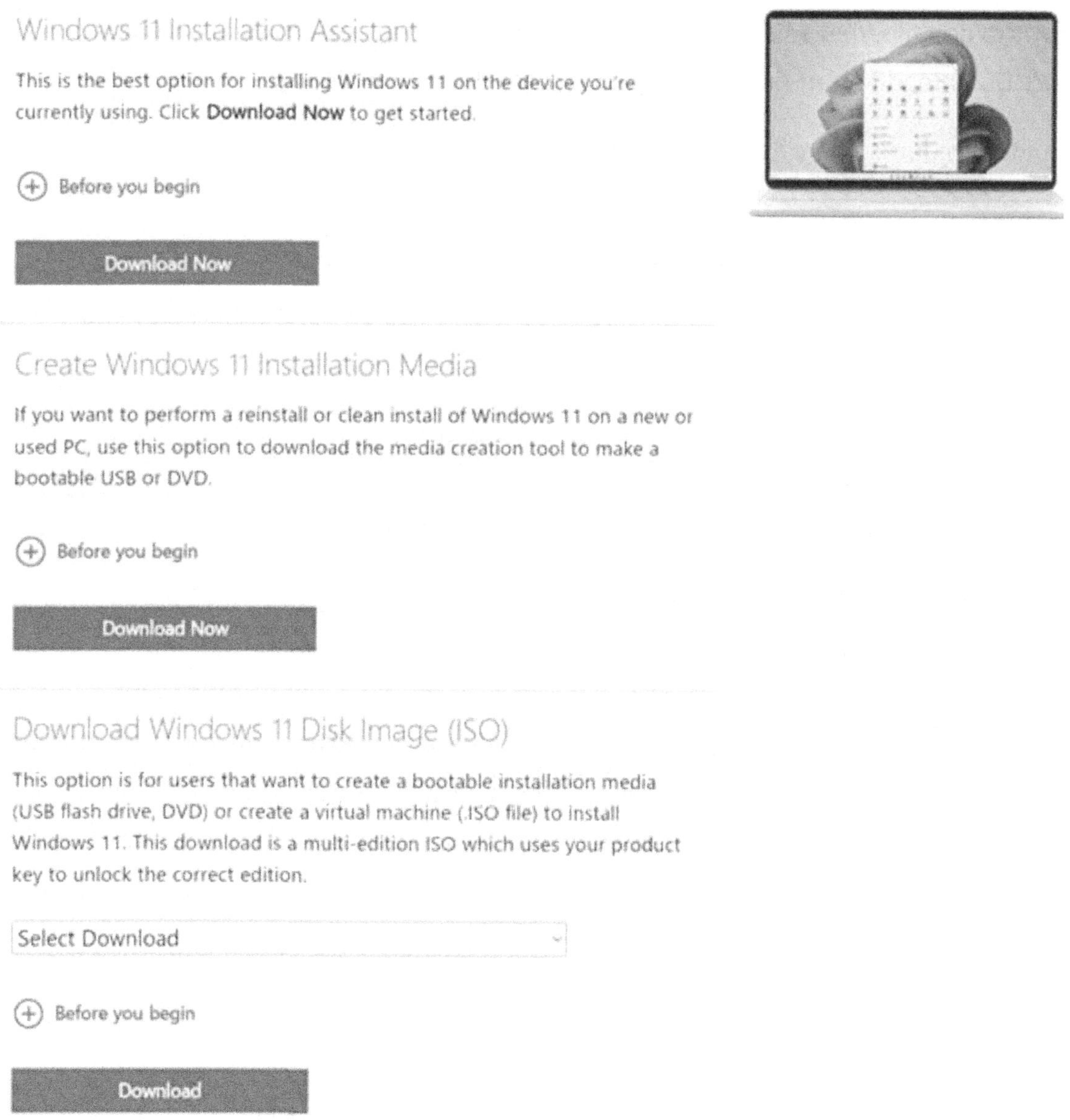

From the above screenshot, you are given three main options through which you can download Windows 11 Operating System software to install later on your PC. The options are: Windows 11 Installation Assistant, Windows 11 Installation Media, and Windows 11 Disc Image (ISO). Out of these three options, we are using the first one on the assumption that your PC meets the requirements needed for Windows 11 installation.

On the Windows 11 download page, under option 1, click the Download Now button. When you click the Download Now button, Microsoft may prompt you to use the PC health check app to determine whether your computer meets the requirements to run Windows 11. Allow it to complete the check. Even if you are not prompted to run the health check at that time, you will be prompted to do so before installing the Windows 11 OS software.

Simply locate the program once it has been downloaded to your computer. If you're not sure where to look for the downloaded software, it should be in the Downloads folder by default. To access your computer's Download folder, first select File Explorer, then Downloads.

The Download folder is one of the folders that is pinned to your computer's Quick Access section by default.

When you open your PC's Downloads folder, look for the Windows 11 program you downloaded. When you get to the program, right-click it and choose Open. As you complete this step, your computer will prompt you to allow the program to make changes to your computer.

Simply press the Yes button. Follow the prompt as you grant your computer's request. The first step may be for you to accept the terms and conditions of the company. Accept it and move forward. Follow the other prompts until the brand-new Windows 11 Operating System is installed on your computer.

Please be patient as Windows 11 installation on your PC may take up to an hour. This is determined by the speed of your computer's processor. In this regard, I recommend that you fully charge your PC battery before beginning the installation. You can also connect your computer to a power source while it is installing. Another thing I want to emphasize is that you should back up any important files on your computer before beginning the installation. This is due to the possibility of file loss during the installation process. Before you begin the installation, simply share the files on Microsoft OneDrive. OneDrive is a dependable cloud storage app developed by Microsoft that allows you to upload files and keep them safe.

CHAPTER 5

HOW TO SETUP MICROSOFT ACCOUNT AND WHAT SERVICES YOU CAN USE WITH IT

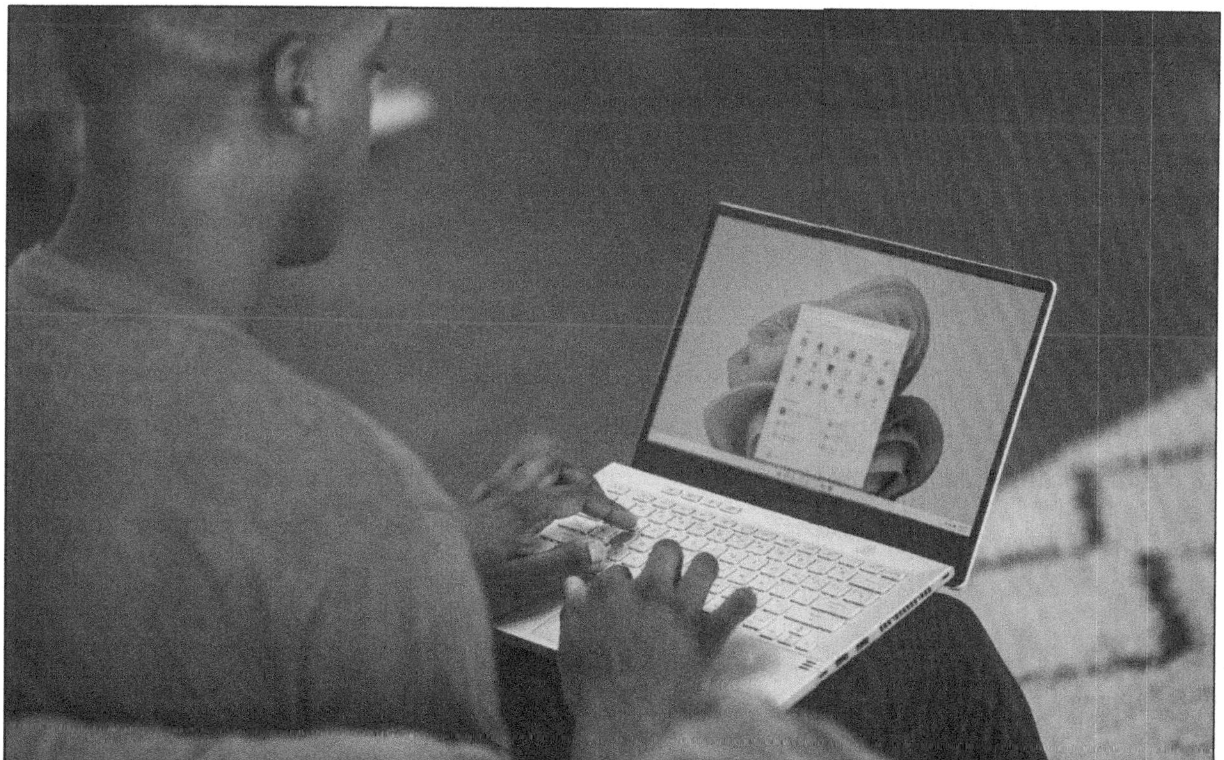

If you have upgraded from Windows 10 and already had a Microsoft account set up, it will be carried across to Windows 11. But if you are starting up a brand-new Windows 11 computer, you will need to set up a new Microsoft account.

What Your Microsoft Account is Used For

A Microsoft account gives you access to a whole suite of Microsoft products, acting as a single sign-in for Office, Xbox Live, Bing, Skype, OneDrive, Windows, Outlook.com and more. If you use multiple computers, using a single account lets you sync and maintain consistency across all devices.

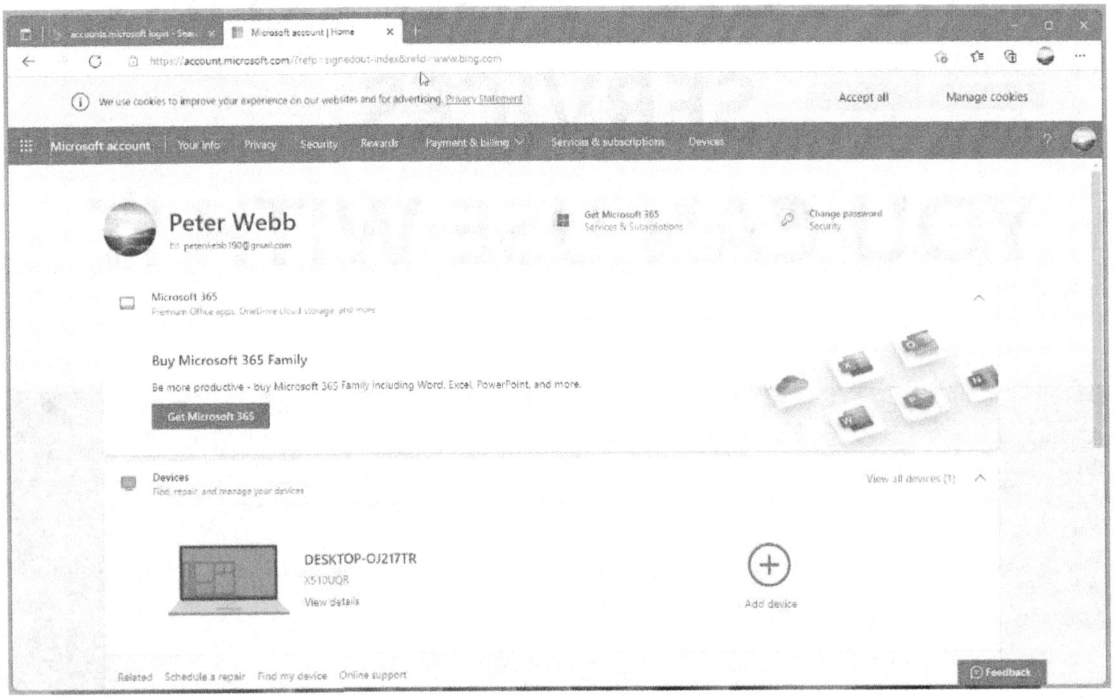

You can use Windows 11 without a Microsoft account, although Microsoft seems to be making this harder to do with each version of Windows it releases. There are good reasons for choosing to use a local account, rather than a normal Microsoft account, but for most new users setting up a Microsoft account is probably the better choice. You can always switch to a local account later if you decide you want to.

Creating Your Account

During the First Time Setup process, if you are using a brand-new computer, you will be prompted to sign in to a Microsoft account. You must first connect your computer to the Internet, after which you will be prompted to sign in to an existing account or create a new one.

1 - Sign in if you already have an account, then complete the rest of the First Time Setup. If not, follow the link to set up a new account.

2 - Enter the email address you'd like to use to access your Microsoft account. This does not have to be a Microsoft email address (live.com, for example), so you can use an existing email address, such as a Gmail account. You can also substitute a phone number for an email address.

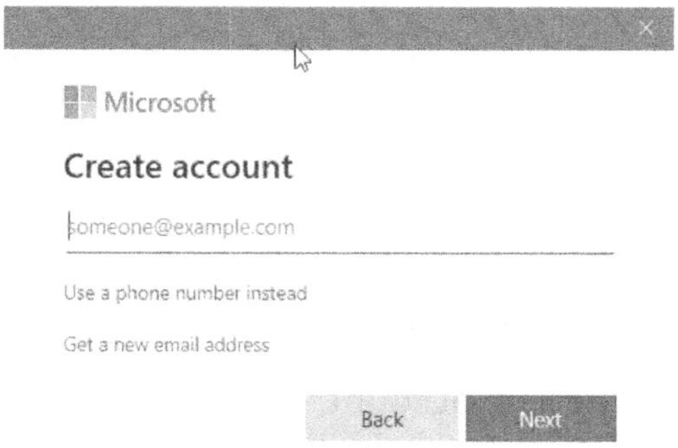

3 - Create a password for your account and then enter the required information (name, date of birth, country, etc.)

4 - If you used an email address, you must confirm the account by entering the code provided in the email. If you provided a phone number, the code will be sent to you via SMS.

To finish setting up your new Microsoft account, follow the remaining instructions on the screen. The Windows 11 installation will proceed once you have signed in.

Changing the Primary Account

Multiple accounts can exist on the same computer, but only the first or primary account is electronically connected to the Windows servers. The primary account has control over all other accounts on a computer.

1 - Go to Settings > Accounts on your computer to check the Primary account. At the top of the Accounts section, the primary account, email, and avatar will be displayed.

2 - Go to the Email & Accounts section to see which other accounts are available in Windows 11. The accounts will be listed in alphabetical order, with the primary account at the top.

3 - To add more accounts, click the "Add account" button and follow the above-described sign-in or setup process. Following that, these accounts will be listed.

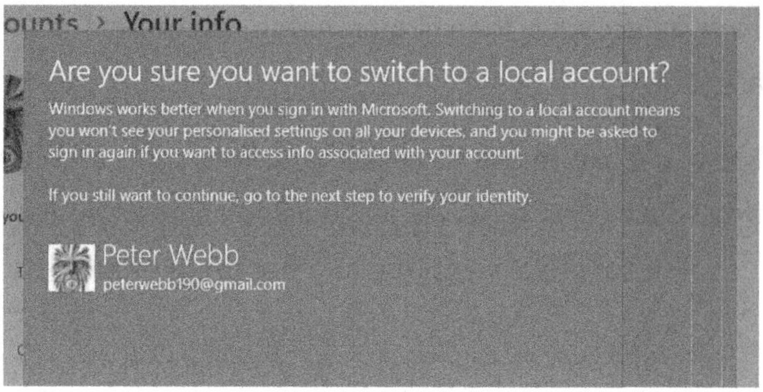

4 - To change the primary account, you must first change to a local account. Go to Accounts > Your Info, and then click "Sign in with a local account instead" under "Account settings."

5 - Follow the instructions to sign out of the existing account and into a local account. You will need to know all of the login details for the primary account, as well as the PIN (if you have set one).

6 - Once this is done, you will see that under "Account Settings", the option is now "Sign in with a Microsoft account instead". Click this and sign in with the new details of the account you want to be the primary account.

7 - Be aware that you may need to change the account that is associated with email, calendar, and other apps for them to work properly. You can do this is Settings > Accounts > Email & Accounts.

CHAPTER 6

INTERNET AND BROWSER SETUP

One of the most important things you can't do without on your PC is to browse the internet; Windows as an operating system is useless if you can't access your favorite websites on it, which is why Microsoft Edge was released with Windows 10. Microsoft Edge is more improved and faster than the one you're used to in Windows 10. This chapter introduces you to various internet operations that you can perform using Microsoft Edge or other Web browsers, as well as various methods of connecting to the internet.

Connecting to the Internet Wirelessly

Tethering is the process of connecting your PC to a nearby Wi-Fi connection in order to browse the internet without using a cable connection. Once you've connected to one of the Wi-Fi networks, your PC is ready to explore the internet.

Are you prepared to connect to a nearby Wi-Fi connection, either private or public? Then you must follow the following guidelines:

To access various types of connections on your PC, take the shortest path by clicking on the "Wi-Fi" icon in the taskbar (you are likely to see two different icons depending on your connectivity).

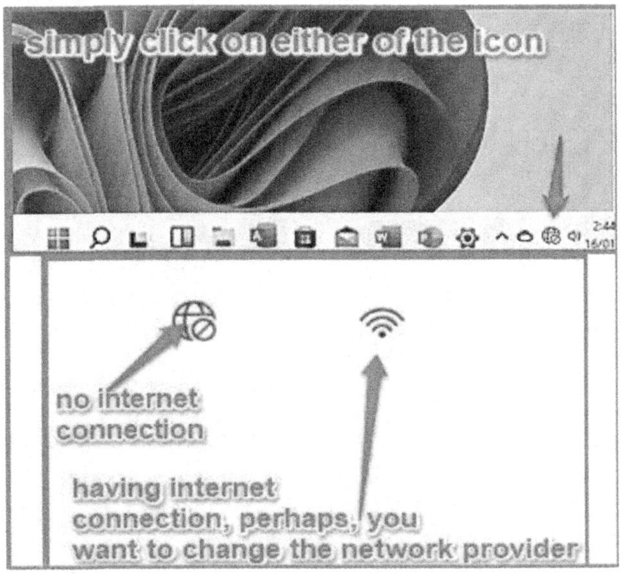

Tap on the “**right arrow**” beside the Wi-Fi icon to access the list of all the nearby wireless networks, Windows is putting the fastest and strongest network to the top.

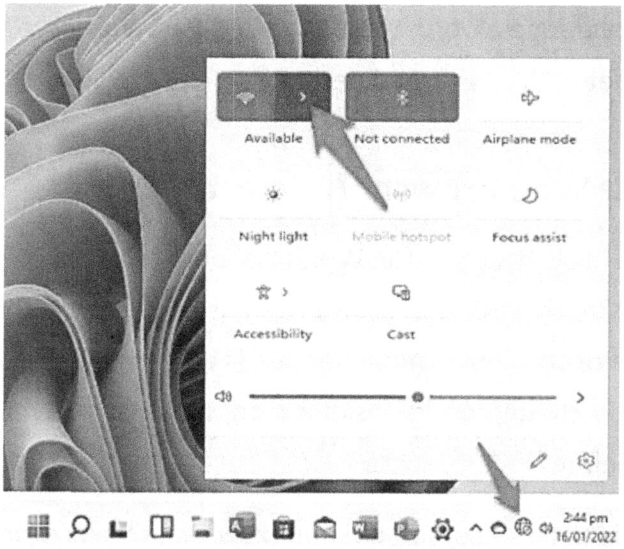

Look for the network name you want, then click "**its name**" and strike on the "**Connect**" button (you may place a mark on the Connect Automatically check the box if it is likely to connect to the same Wi-Fi network again otherwise leave it unchecked).

When you click on the Connect button, one of the following two things will happen: either you are connected with the network if it is an unsecured network or you are prompted to enter the password if it is a secured network. It is advisable to click on the network you know by asking the providers the password to their network, connecting to the unknown network is likely to expose you to the danger of giving out essential information which may be used to dupe you.

Request for the network provider password, then enter the **Password** into the provided box and strike **Enter** key, it may be a free network or charged network.

Browsing Your In-Built Web Browser (Microsoft Edge)

Microsoft Edge is a built-in web browser for Windows that replaces Internet Explorer in previous Windows versions prior to Windows 10. Microsoft Edge has been the preferred web browser for many Windows users because Microsoft's web connection loads quickly and displays its contents boldly. You can access Microsoft Edge by clicking on its taskbar icon, but first you must understand its Tab icon option, which is discussed below:

A click on the Tab icon provides three commands for executing three commands:

- Enable vertical tabs: Move tabs to the left side rather than the top edge, as they were previously.
- Recently closed tabs: Retrieving a recently closed tab.
- Add all tabs to collection: Add all of your open tabs to a collection that you can access with a single click later.

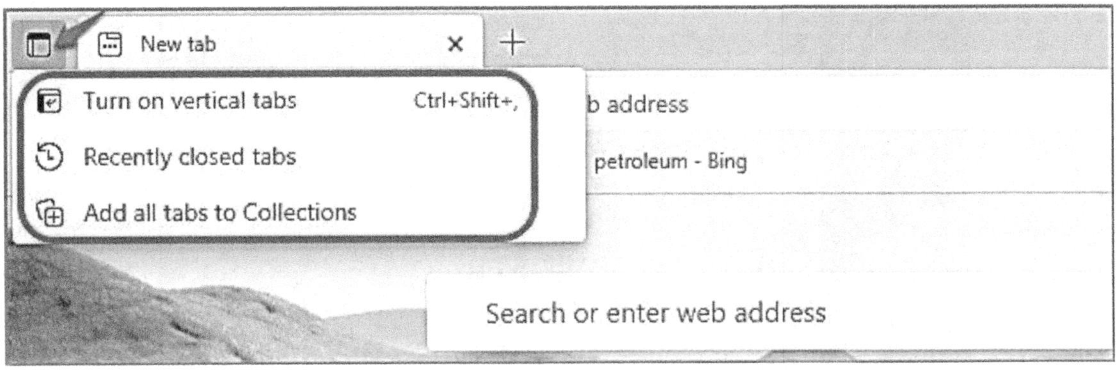

If you plan to use Microsoft Edge, it will be necessary to know the the following points:

1) Tabs action. It represents the tab commands action that we discussed earlier.

2) Tabs: Each tab represents a website that you have opened in your browser.

3) Back button: click this button to return to the previous page you were on.

4) The forward button returns you to the location you left with the back button. Until you press the back button, the forward button is inactive.

5) Refresh button: use this button to reload or refresh a page that isn't loading properly.

6) Address bar: this is the bar or field where you type the URL of the website you want to visit. You can also type anything you want to look up on the internet into this box. It is the address bar for the currently open tab.

7) Open a new tab: clicking this button opens a new tab with an address bar that you can use to visit other websites or search for things.

8) Add this page to favorites: this is the icon for bookmarking the current opening page.

9) Favorite: This is a list of all the website pages you've marked as favorites.

10) Collection: This is the reservoir for the group of tabs you saved with the Tab action; clicking on the Collection will reveal all of the group tabs you saved.

11) Personal: This button allows you to choose whether or not to sync your favorite website with your Microsoft account.

12) Settings and More: this is the button that allows you to print the page, open a new window, change the text on the concerned website, share a site with a friend, and many other things.

Choosing Microsoft Edge Home Page

The Microsoft home page is the display page that appears on the screen when you open Microsoft Edge. Microsoft Edge will always open with the Microsoft website by default, but you can choose any of your favorite websites as the home page. Follow the steps below to make any of your favorite websites your Microsoft Edge home page:

- Open your "**Microsoft Edge**" and click the "**Favorite**" icon to access your favorite websites.

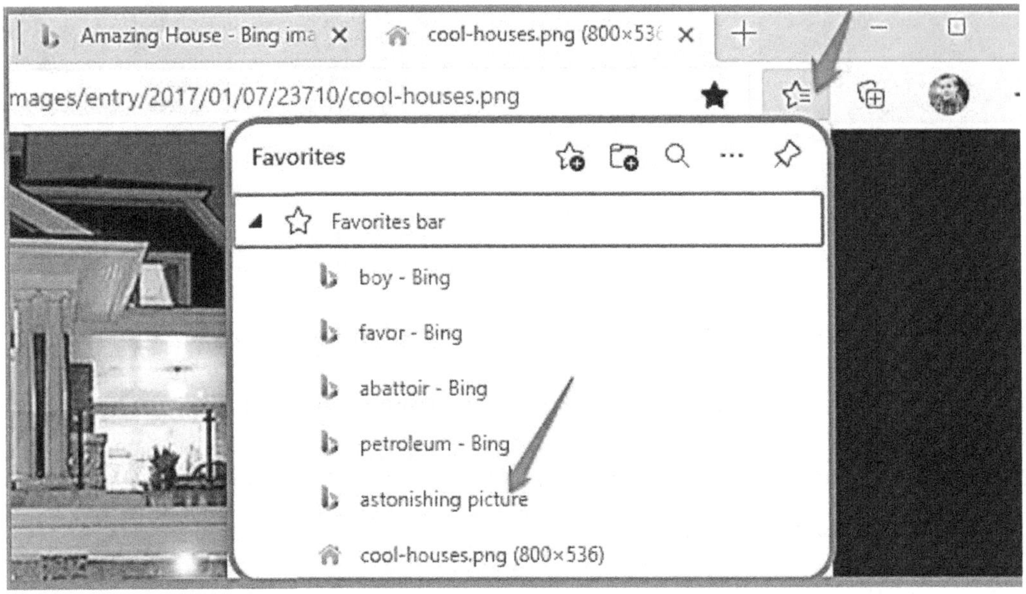

- Click on the particular favorite website you will like to make as the home page from the list of your favorite website and click on the **Settings and More button.**
- Select **Settings** from **Settings and More** fly-out menu to open Settings tab.

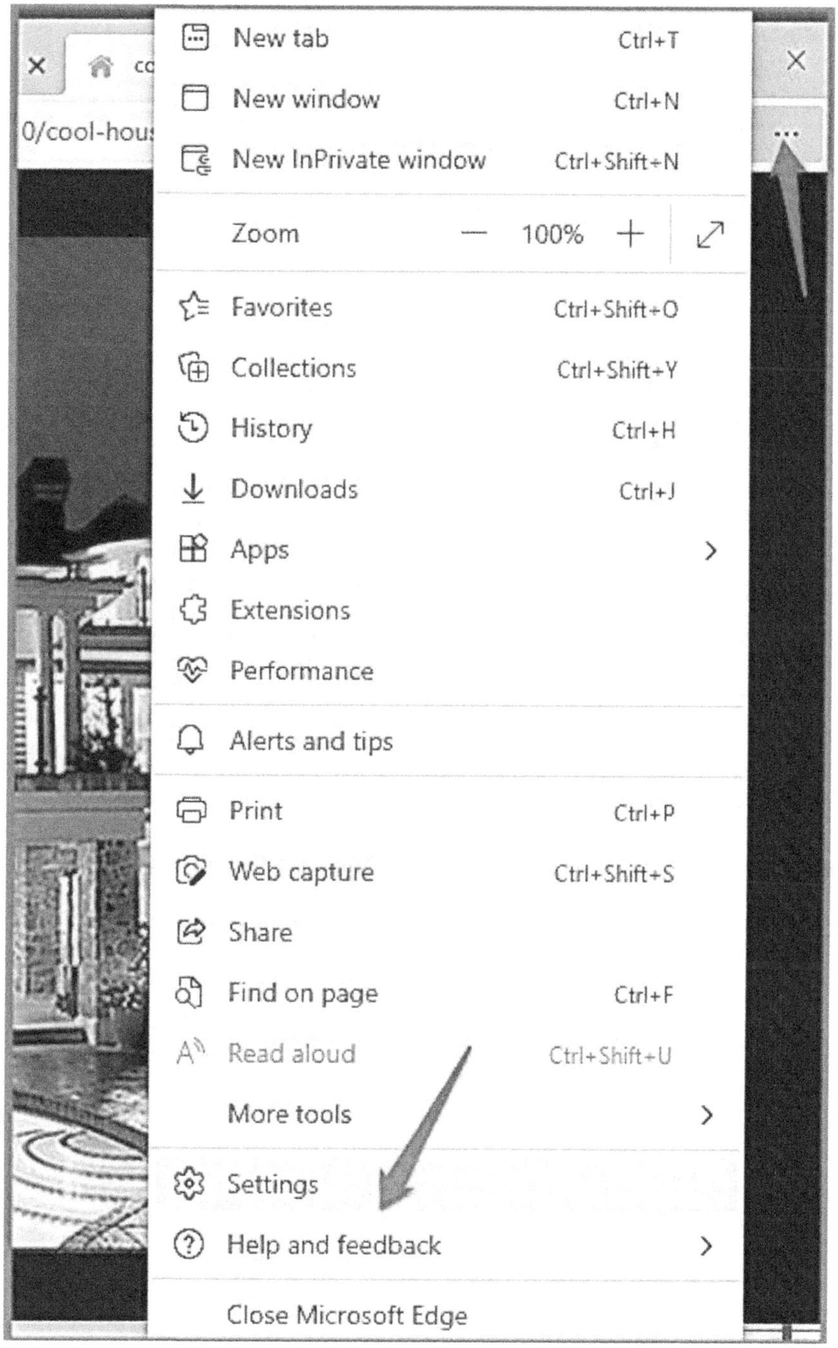

- Click on the "**Start, home and new tabs**" section then move to the "**When Edge starts**" category and click on Use all open tabs to make the currently open favorite website as your Microsoft Edge home page, then click on the X icon at the topmost of the Microsoft Edge to close the Settings tab. When you check your home page, it must have changed to the new home page, and that is what it will be displayed any time you launch into Microsoft edge.

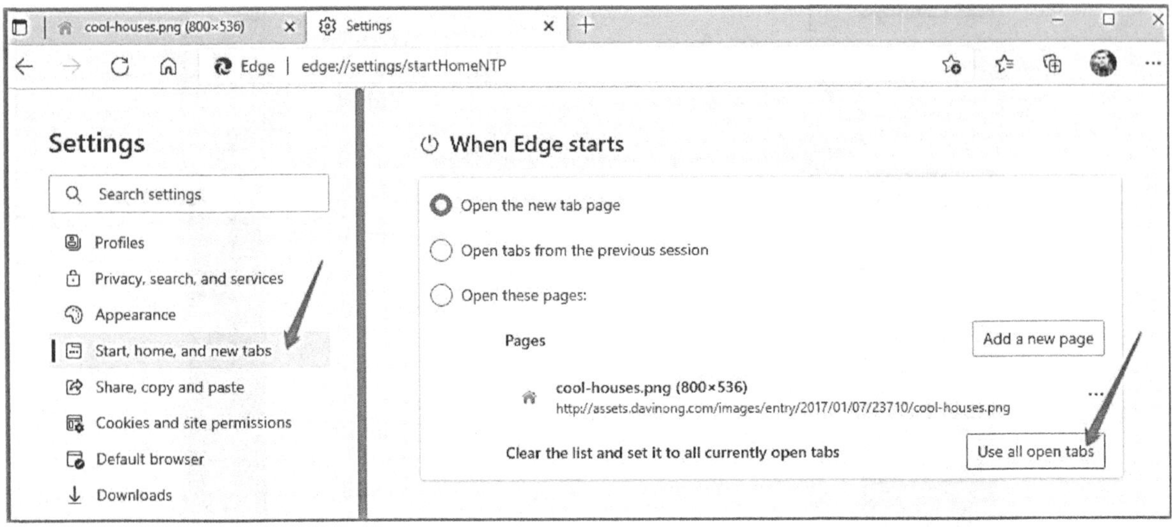

Note: from the home page, you can do all other things just like the default home page and other browsers, for instance, you can browse the internet, enter into the website, search for particular things, and every other thing.

Revisiting Your Favorite Site

The favorite site is worthless until there is a chance of enjoying the same vibe once again. What do you do when you see a favorite site? You save them for another visitation. To add a site into a favorite list, do well to:

i. Tap on the "**Add this page to Favorite"** icon at the right edge of the address bar to access the favorite added box.

ii. You can use the same name or edit it to your desired name and click on the **Done** button to add the page to the favorite list.

iii. Note: To check your favorite place you've previously visited, click on the favorite list icon to access the list of all the favorite sites you've added, then click on the actual one you want to visit again to see that amazing contents once more.

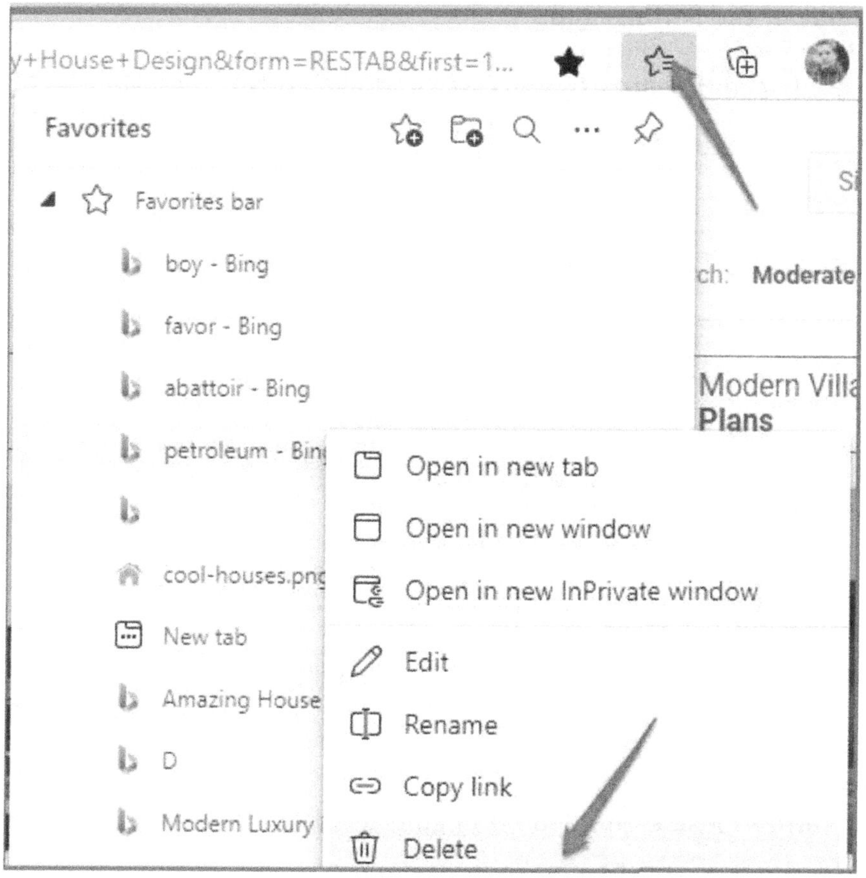

iv. Perhaps some time has passed since you added the previous favorite site to the favorite list; no worries, you can remove it from the favorite list whenever you see that a particular list is no longer of interest to you by right-clicking the offending site's name and selecting Delete from the fly-out list.

Changing The Search Engine For Finding Information

Remember how I told you how to search for things on the Internet? To emphasize, you can search for anything by typing whatever you're looking for into the Address bar and pressing the Enter key to send Windows an errand to find the meaning of that specific information for you.

However, the accuracy and completeness of what you search for is dependent on the search engine that you use. The default search engine of Microsoft Edge is Bing, which is an excellent search engine; however, it may not be your preferred search engine or appropriate for a specific item you want to search for; in that case, please change your search engine by mastering the following steps:

To open Settings on its tab, click the "Settings and More" button in the upper right corner and select "Settings" from the fly-out list.

To access the Privacy, Search, and Services settings category, select "Privacy, Search, and Services" from the upper left side of the Settings tab.

To access the Address bar and Search options, scroll down to the "Service" section and tap on the "Address bar and Search" category.

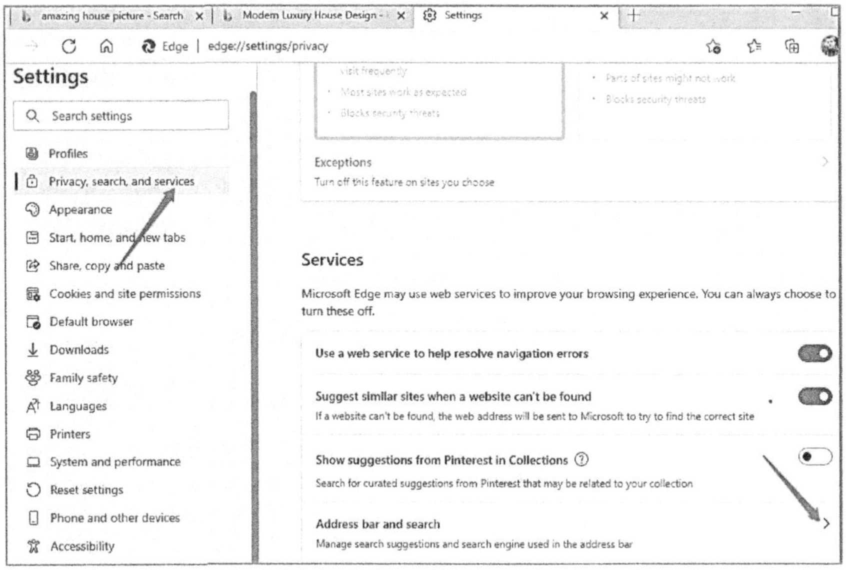

Tap on the **"Down"** arrow beside the Search Engine used in Address Bar and select your desired **"Search Engine"** from the fly-out list to make it a selected search engine for searching for things on the internet. Close the Settings tab by clicking the X on its right side.

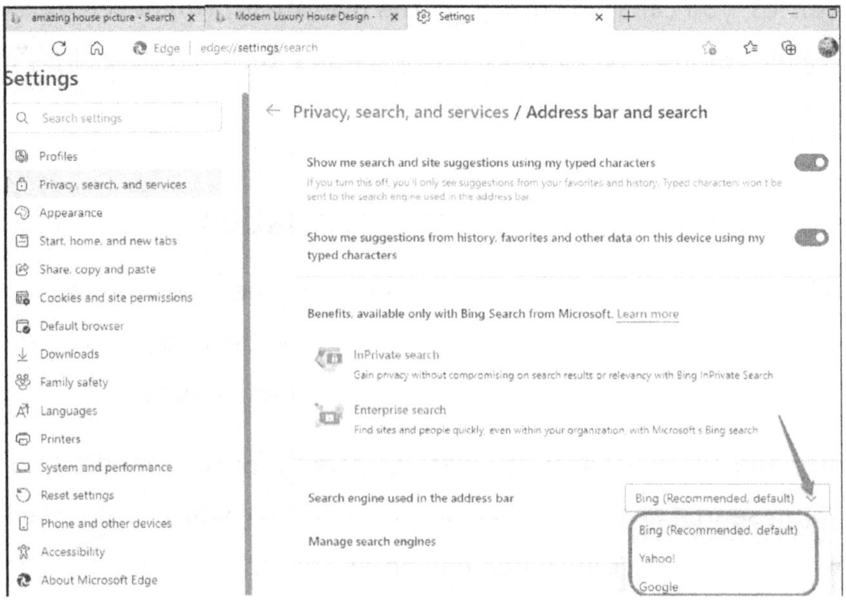

CHAPTER 7

FOLDER ORGANIZATIONS AND PROPERTIES MANAGEMENT

File Explorer is one of the most important applications in Windows 11. This is a tool included with Windows OS that allows users to open all files on a computer system. This is the app we'll be using to open files. However, as a new Windows 11 user, you will be surprised by the new changes in the new File Explorer.

In this portion, I'll show you what's new and how to use it. Of course, you can open the file explorer by clicking the pinned icon in the taskbar, or you can bring this shortcut to your desktop by right-clicking on an empty space on your desktop and selecting Personalize.

Scroll down and click on Themes, then click on the Desktop icon settings, select Computer, and then click Apply and OK.

As can be seen in Windows 11, compared to Windows 10, we have different icons for our partitions, folders, quick access folders, other network stuff, drives, OneDrive, and so on; this is the design aspect which I think is nice.

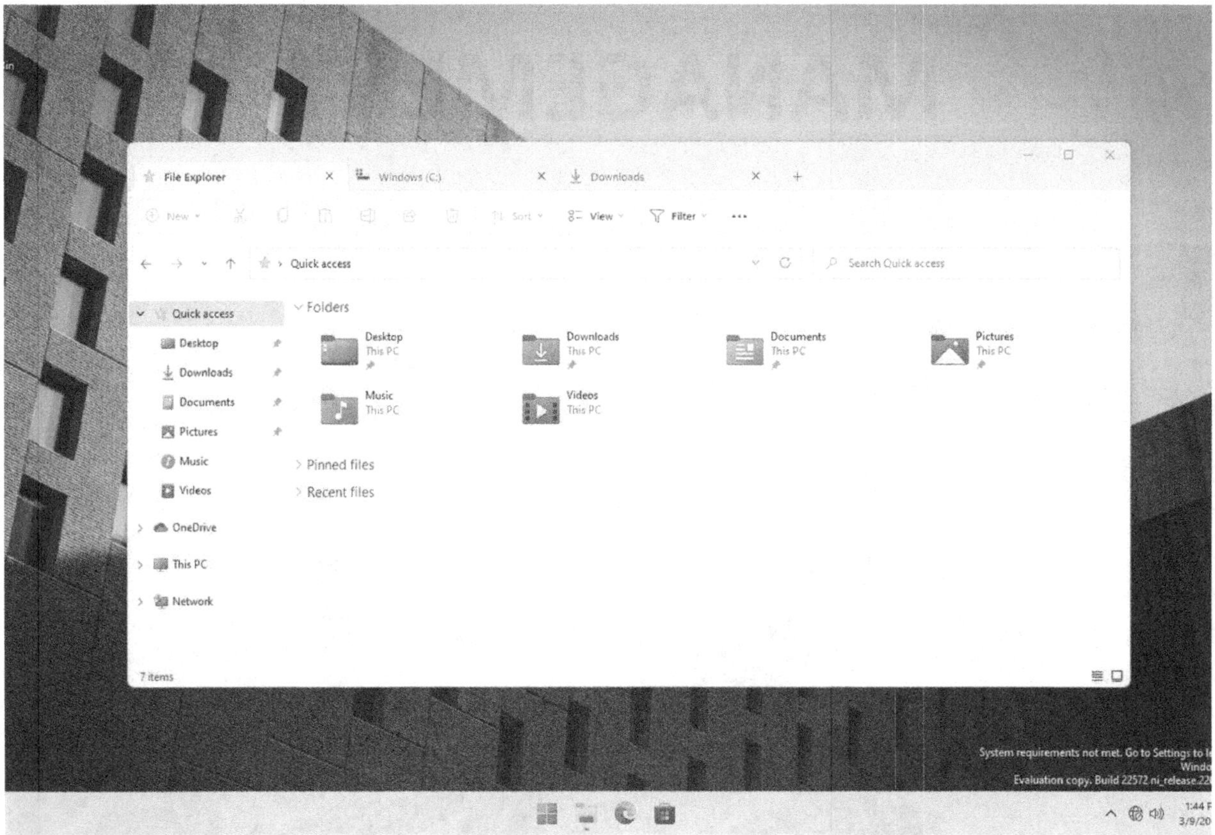

Organizing Things with the File Explorer

Do you know how Windows 11's file explorer works? Do you know where the default file folder is and how it is organized? The file explorer in Windows 11 is significantly different than it was in Windows 10. I'll go over everything in detail with you so you can learn everything quickly.

If we go into a partition, we can see that the new folder icon is a more minimalistic design with more space between the folders, and the section upward in Windows 11 has been changed. When we click on File, we can see all of the available buttons.

When you click on the New tab, it will open this menu where you can create a new folder or a new item, which can be a folder, a shortcut, or a bitmap image. We have the Cut option, the Copy option, the Paste option, and the Rename option to rename a file.

Also included is a Share button, from which we can email a contact or share with an app. It displays our email clients in the section for sharing with an app. Of course, there's the Recycle button, which will move this item to the recycle bin. It will not be permanently removed.

We can sort our files by name, date modified, type, size created, authors, categories, tags, title, as well as in an ascending or descending order which we can group by the same categories, using the sort and group options. We can change the layout of our apps or switch to extra-large icons by using the layout and view options.

We also have a compact view, which will revert our Windows 11 File Explorer to the old Windows 10 File Explorer, which had smaller spaces between files and Quick Access icons and, in my opinion, is not as appealing as Windows 11.

There's also the Show tab, which opens a section where you can show and hide panes. We have the details pane, the preview pane, and the item tick boxes, which are the same as the check boxes in Windows 10.

Of course, you can preview files; this preview feature is limited to images and the like. The details pane displays a wealth of information. This is really cool, in my opinion, because it shows us details without requiring us to right-click and then select Properties.

By clicking on a file, we only see its important details. When we click on a.rar or a.zip file, we have the option to extract everything, and we also have these three dots on the right that allow us to compress the zip file and copy the path of the file, which is very useful.

You can Select all, Select none, Invert selection, Undo the Delete of the previously deleted file, Properties, and Options, which will open the old Windows 10 menu.

I really like the new layout and the new categorized options in Windows 11. I believe they will help Windows 11 users be more productive. And, of course, it's visually appealing.

When we right-click on a file, we have the same options as when we left-clicked on it: Cut, Copy, Rename and Delete, Open, Opening Windows, New Window, Pin to Quick Access, Pin to Start Compressed Zip File, Copy as path, Properties, and Open in Windows terminal, which will open up Windows PowerShell.

The Show More options option brings up the old Windows 10 contextual menu. So that's how you can set up the new Windows 11 File Explorer.

Making Folders

In a computer file system, a folder is a virtual container. Individual files and folders comprise the file system. This may appear complicated to you, but it is a straightforward concept: a folder is a virtual container for files. Consider a folder to be an envelope. It can hold documents or other types of files, but the folder itself is empty when first created.

On a computer, you can have multiple folders that are stored in different locations on the hard drive or storage device. When you see a folder, it means there are many files or data inside. It is critical to understand that the contents of folders are only visible to you and other people who have access to that folder. This is a critical feature to keep in mind when protecting the privacy of your data.

This is a quick tutorial on how to make folders in Windows 11. It's a straightforward procedure with only a few steps to follow.

1. Launch File Explorer and navigate to the folder where you want to save the file.

2. At the top of the screen, click "New Folder."

3. Give the folder a name (this should be the name you'll use to refer to it).

And there you have it! In Windows 11, you now have a new folder.

CHAPTER 8

SETUP AND CUSTOMIZE START MENU WITH FOLDERS AND WIDGETS

The Start menu is one of the advantages of using Windows 11. With the removal of the Apps section, the menu is now a little more intuitive. It's not much of a benefit, because the Start menu is still in the same place, albeit with some new features and a redesigned search box.

However, there are a few things that the start menu allows you to do that the apps view does not. Continue reading if you want to learn more about the new Windows interface.

How To Use Windows 11's Start Screen Menu

One of the first things you'll notice about Windows 11's Start menu is that the background color has been changed. Although Windows 10 had a different background color than the previous versions, you could still change it. It's now black in Windows 11, which should make it easier to see what you're doing. While this is a minor change, having a single background color across the Start menu and other parts of Windows makes a lot of sense.

Open the Settings app to change the background color. Colors can be found under Personalization. Select the color you want by clicking the More Colors button.

Restore The Traditional Start Menu

The removal of the Apps section from the Windows 11 Start menu is one of the more noticeable changes. This is a departure from Windows 10, where you could search for apps as usual. While the classic Windows start menu had a search box, it was Windows 7's search box. This means you couldn't use it to find your apps. You can't use it now that the Apps section is gone. Instead, you get a tile for each app that is installed on your system. There is no longer a need for a separate section for this.

Even though you can't search for apps anymore, the classic start menu still allows you to access the apps you use frequently. The look of the start menu in Windows 11 has changed slightly. Go to the section on the new Windows 11 Start menu to learn how they work.

If you don't like the new look of the start menu, you have a few options. You can return to the previous appearance by going to Settings. The classic start menu remains in Windows 11, as it did in Windows 10. You'll just be able to access it through Settings. Furthermore, if you dislike the appearance of the start menu in Windows 11, you can change the appearance of the Apps section. Simply go to Settings and look for the option to change your App icon.

How to Change the Start Screen

Windows 11 includes new features such as Windows Holographic and a new screen experience. The Start Screen and the Metro screen are no longer available because the Windows desktop has been replaced by the modern desktop. However, the new Modern UI still includes a Start Menu that you can personalize.

You may not even be aware that you can customize the Start screen if you are new to Windows. This is a feature found on the Start screen that is only available in Windows 10. If you do not already have Windows 10, you may not have access to this feature.

However, in the most recent version of Windows, you can remove the Start menu, and the Start screen has become the only screen. You might not realize that the Start screen is also customizable, but here's how to customize the Start screen in Windows 11.

Navigate to the start screen.

To begin, navigate to the Start screen, which will be the only place where you will see the modern Start screen. This can be found by pressing Windows key + S and then typing start.

You can also access the Start screen by clicking the Start button.

When you open the Start screen, two options will appear next to the Microsoft logo. You can navigate to a new settings screen by selecting the Settings option. When you select the Store option, you will be taken to another screen where you can configure your Store account.

The modern search option appears on the following screen. When you click on the new icon, Windows will launch the search interface.

Modify the appearance of your start screen.

You need to change the appearance now that you've reached the modern start screen.

You must first select the More tab, then scroll down to the Settings option. You will then be presented with options such as Time and Language, Privacy, Location, and Screen Savers.

To change the background of the Start screen, select Screen Saver from the new dropdown menu.

The Screen Saver option on the following screen allows you to customize your Start screen background, Windows theme, and screen saver. If you want to add a new background, click on the Screen Saver icon and choose the one you want.

If you don't like the icons on your Start screen, click the App Icons link and then select the apps you want.

To change the tile on your Start screen, click the Small Apps link. The following screen is called Tile Settings, and it allows you to select which apps you want to display as tiles.

Click on the Lock screen link to change your Lock screen. You can choose the tiles, the color of the text, and how long you want to be locked.

To change the color of your Start screen, click the Colors link and then scroll down to see a list of available colors. To select a color, click on the Color palette link and select the desired color.

Click on the Desktop link to change your desktop background.

Click the Log on Screen Settings link to change the background of each of your Log on screens.

How to Use the Search Capability on the Start Screen

The problem is that the Start screen is NOT designed for searching. It's just a loading screen. It's not really intended to have built-in searching. You're used to having the search box, which is normally found on the Start Menu, inside the Taskbar and can then be launched from both the start screen and directly from there.

There is now another way to find things. Instead of the start screen, Windows includes a built-in search app. To access it, navigate to the Start Screen and press the Windows key, followed by the 'X' key. If you press the Windows key, it will appear at the top right of the start screen. 'Search Windows,' it says.

If you must use the start screen, simply open a folder from the start screen. You won't be able to search inside, but it is possible.

How to Change the Sounds

To set a custom sound as the default, right-click on the "Sound" option on the taskbar's left side and select "Set as default sound."

If you want to replace the default sounds with a custom sound, right-click on the "Sound" option on the taskbar's left side and select "Set as custom sound." To disable it, navigate to Settings>Sounds and Audio Devices>Sound and change the setting to "Normal."

In Windows 11, you can add folders to the Start Menu.

In Windows 11, you can add folders to the Start Menu in the same way that you can in Windows 10. On the Settings > Personalization > Start page, select "Folders."

You can personalize the Start Menu by adding folders such as Downloads, Documents, Pictures, and more.

The folders will be located to the left of the power menu in the Start Menu. This way, you can quickly access important folders from the Start menu in Windows 11, without having to navigate through pinned applications or anything else.

With Windows 11, you can also add a custom folder to the Start menu. Right-click on the folder and select "Pin to Start" from the drop-down menu. (Note: You do not need to use any third-party applications or modify the App Data folder because the new OS allows you to pin folders to the Start Menu by default.)

The custom folder will now be visible in the Start Menu's "Pinned" applications area. (This function may assist you in keeping your desktop tidy and free of clutter.)

Microsoft has also added the option to move the Start Menu and other taskbar icons to the left side of the screen. Under Settings > Personalization > Taskbar, select "Left" from the new "Taskbar alignment" option.

Widgets

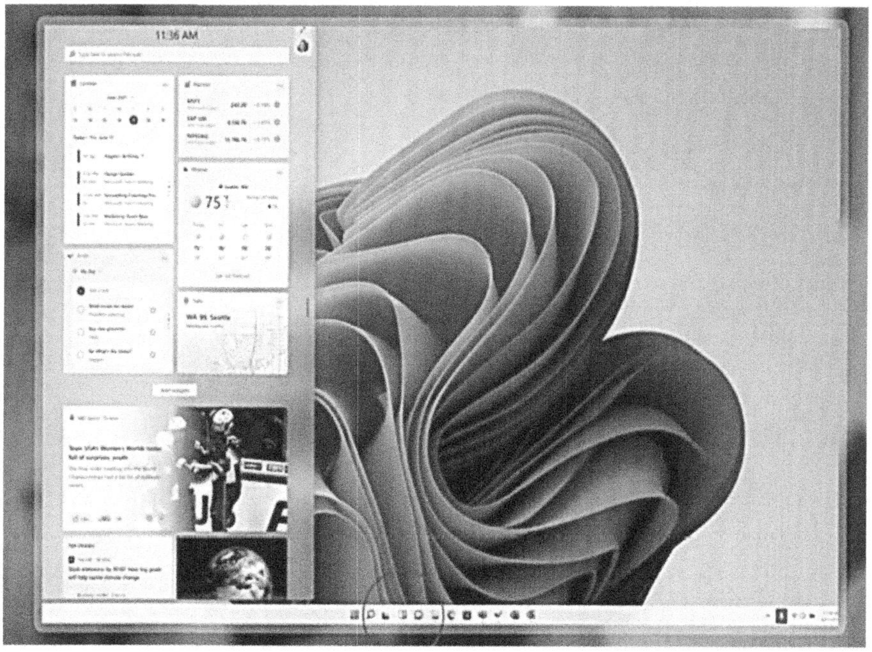

The widget icon is next in line on the taskbar. You can now view your important updates using this feature. You'll find the weather, news and calendar widget. You can also add new widgets as well for more diversity. To do this;

- Click the widget icon (the fourth icon on the taskbar). This will bring up a widget panel on the left side of the screen.
- On touch screen laptops, you can also bring up the widget by swiping from the left side. Simply tap on the screen to remove it.
- Select a new widget by clicking Add widgets.

- You can also change the size of a widget by clicking the options icon in the widget box's top right corner. Choose between small, medium, and large widget sizes.
- To remove a widget, click the options icon in the upper right corner of the widget box and select remove widget.
- To search the web, use the search field at the top of the widget page.

CHAPTER 9

HOW TO MANAGE DISK STORAGE

The one precise setting that Windows 10 usually lacked was the availability of the right disk management setting within the Windows Settings. Windows 11 fills that hole with the right disk control tools as a feature in the Windows Settings. Users can now examine the storage power and control the disk storage without leaving the Settings window.

Exploring Storage Devices

- Go to Settings or press Windows key + I at the same time
- Select System settings
- Select Storage option
- Click on Advanced Storage Settings
- Scroll down to Disk & Volumes to explore and analyse devices

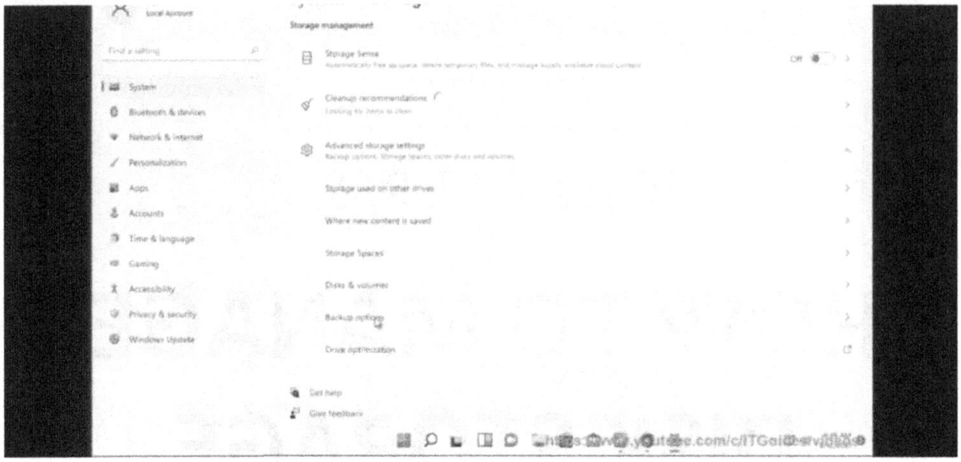

Here, all active storage drives can be viewed and managed, including the PC's main storage and all external storages. The storage devices active on the computer can be expanded, viewed, and managed right from the Settings window.

- Navigate, click and select the dropdown icon of the storage drive wished to be managed and expanded
- Select the specific drive and click Explore

This would bring up all things contained in the drive storage as in File Explorer.

Increasing and Decreasing Drive Partition Size

- Follow steps 1-7 in the previous section, but instead of clicking Explore, select Properties
- Select Change Size

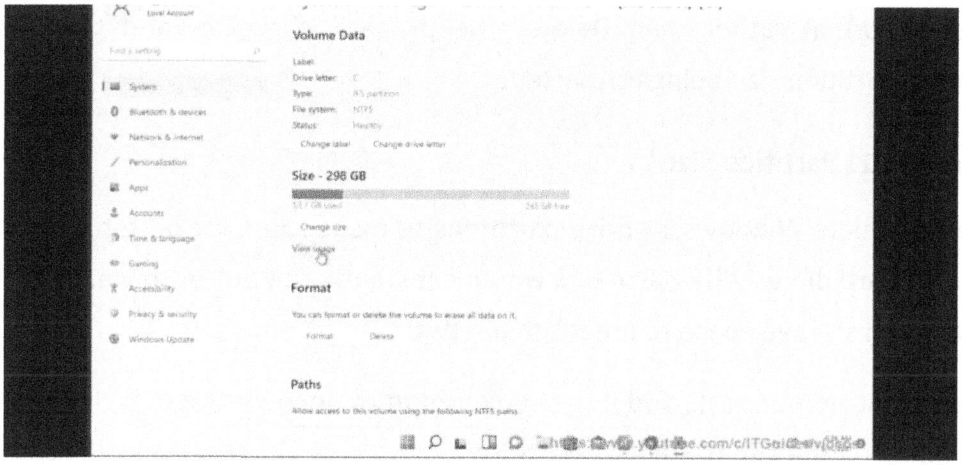

A window would then pop up from where the partition size can be edited. It is labelled in MB(Megabytes). This would require just a bit of calculation;

For example, say the current partition size allocation is 20GB and a user wants to increase it to maybe 50GB, converting to MB:

$50 \times 1024 = 51{,}200$MB

This value is what would be entered in the said pop up window.

- Click OK

The transformation does not happen overnight. The computer takes its time to make the change, which is also affected by the size difference between the old and new partition sizes.

When reducing the size of any storage partition in Windows 11, the same steps must be followed.

Viewing Storage Utilization

- Repeat the first step for changing drive partition size, but instead of selecting Change Size, select View Usage.
- A view of the drive and all folders contained within it, as well as the storage space occupied by the files, would appear. These folders can also be expanded to access specific files by simply clicking on them.
- Perform the preceding steps to gain access to any drive after deleting or formatting a partition.
- At thc bottom of thc window, click the Delete button.

When all subsequent instructions on pop-up windows are followed and completed, this action completely erases the partition or drive.

To format, select Format rather than Delete. The process is similar, and the time required is determined by the partition size being formatted.

Managing Windows 11 Partition Size

Users can resize or delete Windows 11 drive partitions to make room for better drive storage, usage, and management. Hard drives' disk partitions would constantly run out of space. This is because they may not have enough storage space to meet the needs of users.

Partition resizing is a common task, and it is also common to encounter issues. It could take hours to complete depending on the size of the disk partition.

When drive storage space runs out, the PC will display the "Low Disk Space" error message. Fortunately, Windows 11 allows you to shrink or expand a partition to make room for more storage space. This process is known as shifting or moving a disk partition.

In addition to creating, deleting, and formatting partitions, Disk Management, a built-in tool in Windows, can manage and edit allotted partitions without causing users to lose data. However, because of its numerous limitations, Disk Management is not the best tool for resizing a Windows 11 partition. Actually, Disk Management can only be used to shrink a partition to make more storage space, or to expand a partition by deleting a right contiguous one. Disk Management is ineffective if a user needs to expand one partition by shrinking another.

To shrink Windows 11 partition;

- Press Windows + X keys collectively and then click on Disk Management.

- Right click on any NTFS partition and choose Shrink Volume.

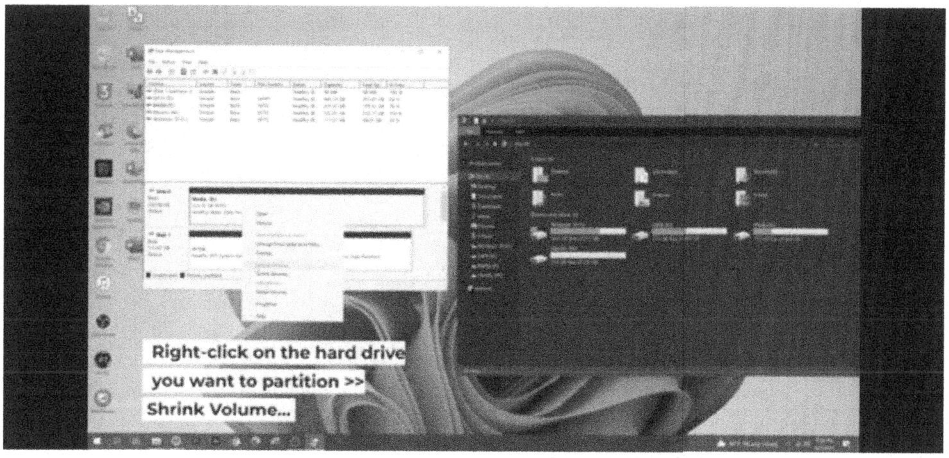

- Enter desired amount of storage space, calculated as earlier explained after which click on Shrink button.

- If no value is entered, Windows then by default allocates the maximum storage space that can be utilized.

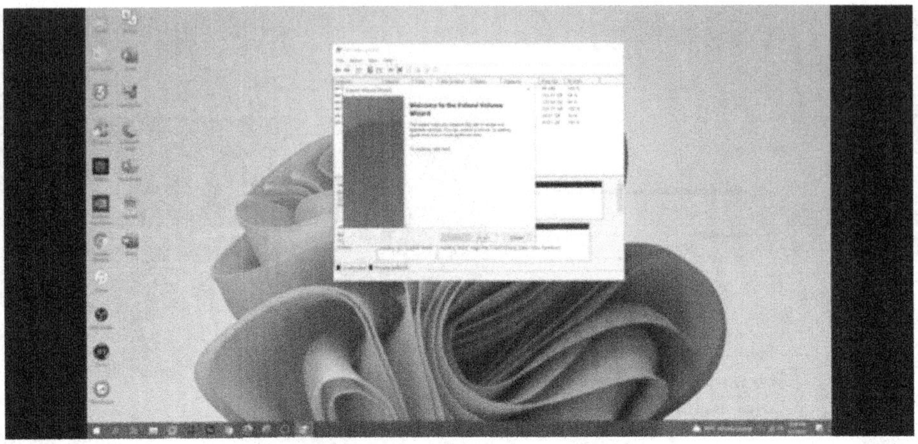

- Simply follow the instructions on Extend Volume Wizard window to complete the action.

To extend Windows 11 partition;

- Backup all documents in for instance drive D: (the right contiguous partition) to different storage location.
- Right click on this partition and choose Delete Volume, the disk area would then be modified to Unallocated.

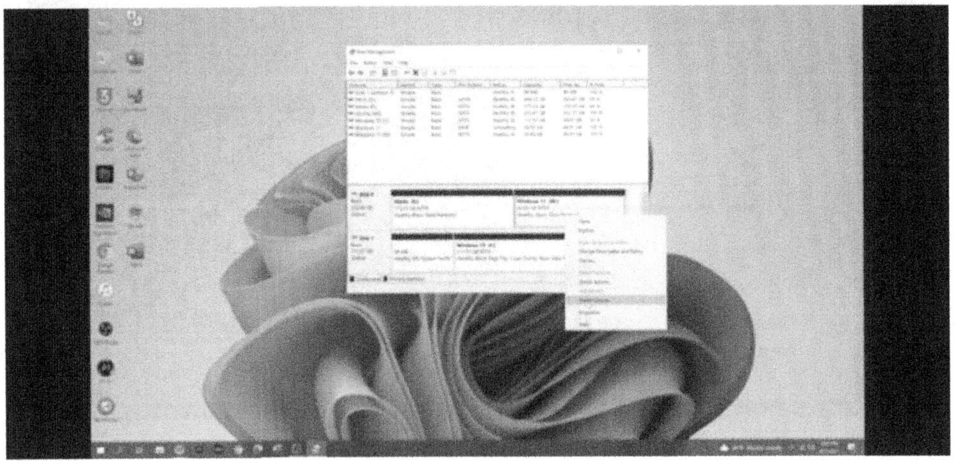

- Right click on the left contiguous partition (for instance C:) and choose Extend Volume.

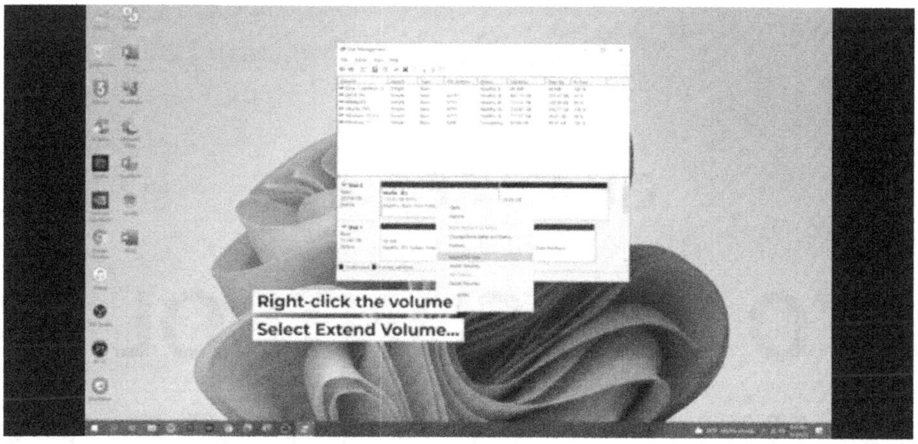

- Simply follow the instructions on Extend Volume Wizard window to complete the action.

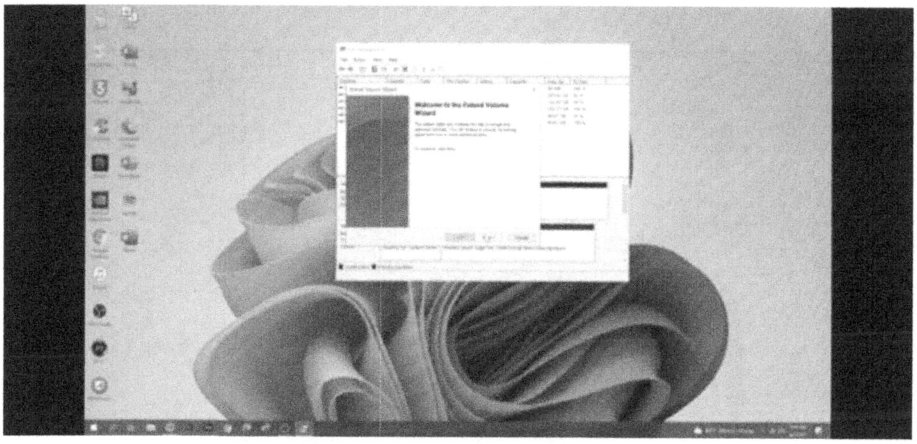

Windows Disk Management tool can only be used for resizing NTFS storage partitions; FAT32 and any other storage types cannot be managed or modified with Disk Management.

CHAPTER 10

HOW TO USE CONTROL PANEL & UNINSTALL PROGRAMS

How To Navigate The Control Panel In Windows 11

Windows 11's engine is the Control Panel. Although Microsoft is touting the new and improved Settings app in the new OS, the classic Control Panel is in the same role. There's a reason it's still in the operating system. And the reason for this is that Microsoft has yet to transition away from all of the features and options available here. The Control Panel still has a plethora of advanced settings, such as hardware troubleshooting, backup and restore, internet and power options, sound, color management, and so on.

Control Panel Access

There are multiple ways to launch Control Panel in Windows 11, as well as multiple ways to use it. The Settings app contains scattered direct links to specific Control Panel applets, indicating the importance of the classic Control Panel.

Although personalization and customization options are available in both Settings and Control Panel, the latter now primarily contains legacy options. This migration is still ongoing in Windows 11, so the classic Control Panel will remain in the OS for the foreseeable future.

From the Start Menu, select Control Panel.

This panel can be launched by performing a simple search in the Start Menu. Not only can you open it from here, but you can also launch the most recently opened applets from there.

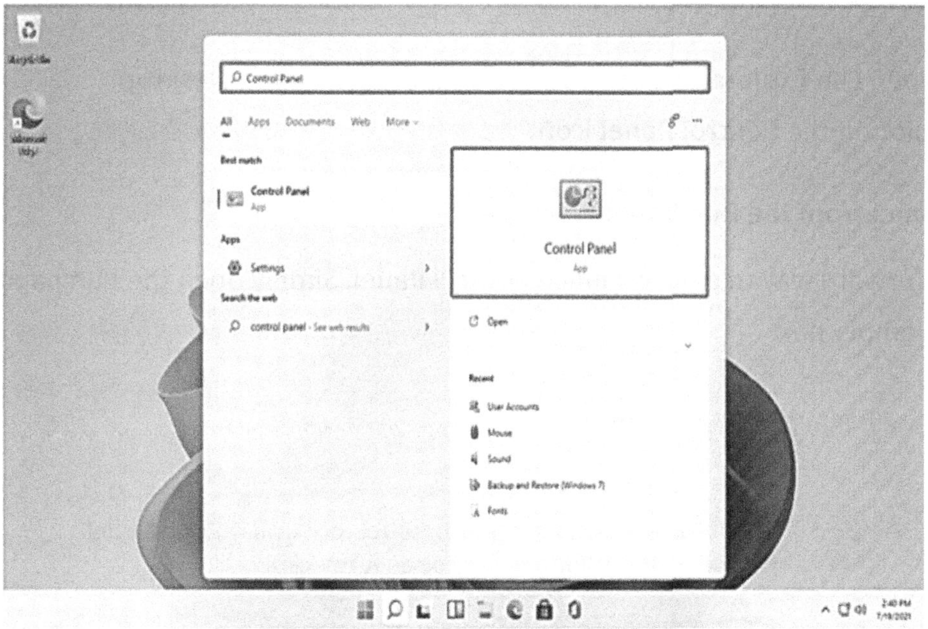

- Click on **Search** from the screen and inside the box type **Control Panel**.
- Then either you hit the Enter key or click the icon.

Open Control Panel from File Explorer

A shortcut to the Control Panel lies in the File Explorer, though not where you might expect it. Once you are on the Desktop, you will find an icon for the Control Panel next there.

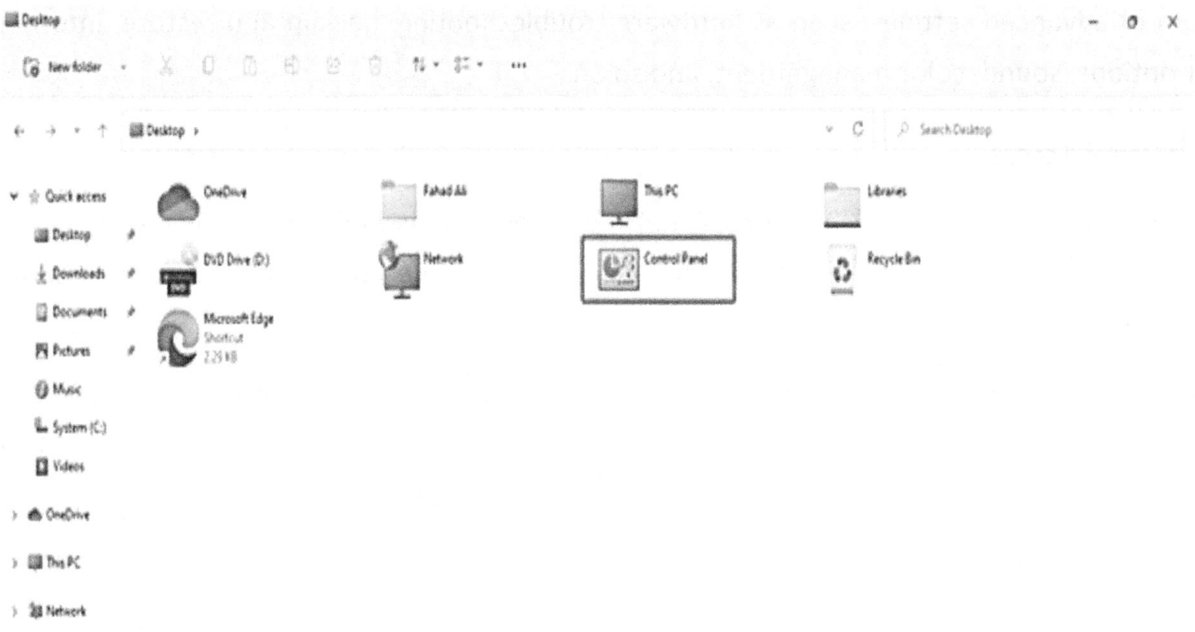

- Click to open **File Explorer**, hover the mouse, and click on the **Desktop**,
- Double-click on the **Control Panel** icon.

Open Control Panel from the Run Panel

This is a straightforward way to quickly launch Control Panel. Simply open the Run panel and then type the name in the empty box.

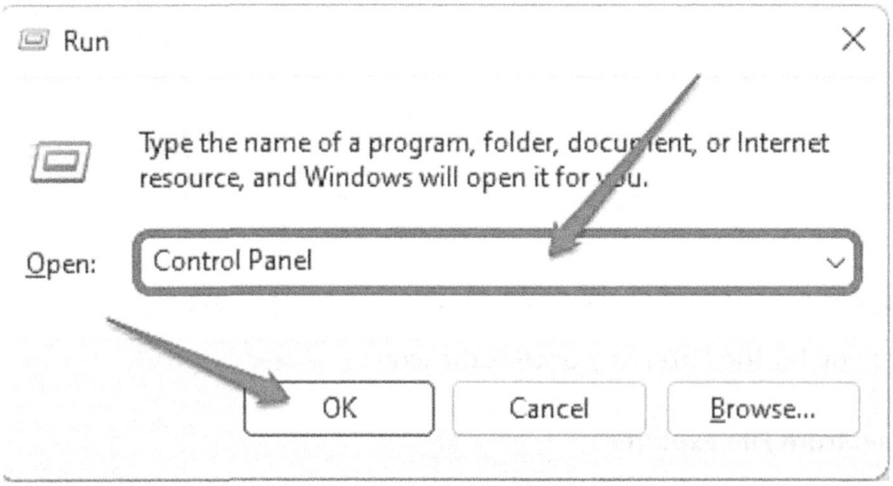

From your keyboard press **Window logo + R** to open the Run dialogue, enter the **control panel**, and hit **Enter** or click **OK**.

How to Uninstall Applications in Windows 11

Sometimes, we install some apps that we want to use temporarily on our PC. After some time, we may like to remove these apps completely from our PC. But if we do not know how to go about this, it becomes a problem. To uninstall an app is to remove an application from a computer. When you uninstall an app, you free up some space on your PC.

To uninstall an app from your PC, click the **Search** icon at the taskbar of your PC running Windows 11 and then type "app" in the Search space. From the results that will show up, click on **Add or remove programs**. The photo below explains that.

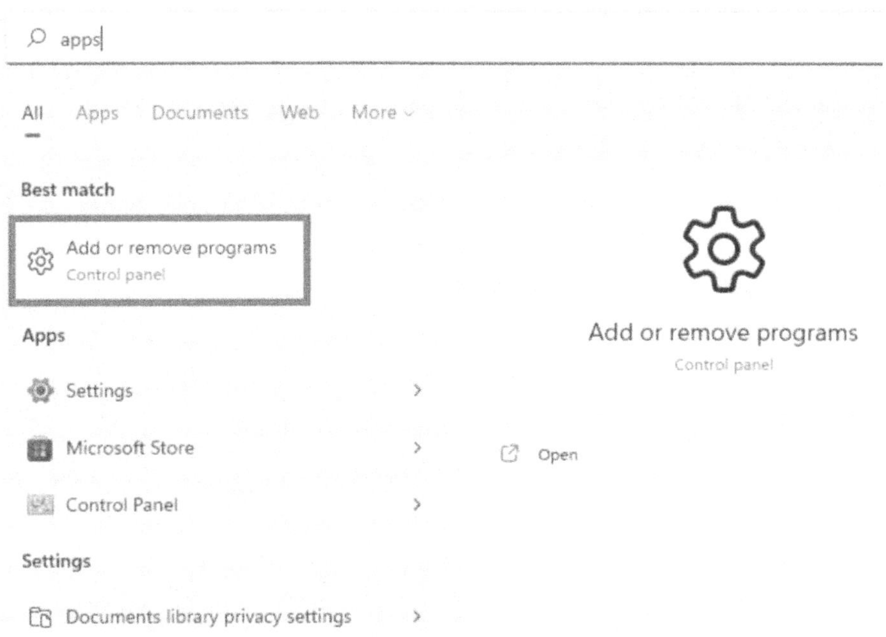

A new page will open on your PC once you click the **Add or remove programs**. You will see all the apps that are installed on your Windows 11 computer. When you get to any of the app you want to uninstall from your PC, click the ellipsis (the three dots on it) and lastly select **Uninstall**. The photo below shows options you will see on clicking the ellipsis.

The app gets uninstalled from your PC within a few seconds.

Note: There are some other ways that can get you to the apps on your computer from where you can uninstall any you do not want to have on your computer again.

CHAPTER 11

FILES MANAGEMENT AND SHORTCUTS TO USE

In this new chapter, I will continue teaching you for you to know more on the latest Operating System used by Windows computers.

Moving Files in a Folder

One thing is to create a folder, and another is to copy files that were existing before into the created folder. There are many ways through which you can move files into a folder you created on your PC.

You can move file to a folder by first selecting the file (you can select a file by just a click on it). When the file is selected, right-click on the file to see some options, and among the options click **Copy** icon. This is explained in the photo below.

Another quicker way to copy a file is through shortcut. To do that, just select the file by giving it just a click. Then, press **Ctrl** and **C** key of your computer keyboard. When you do this, the file you selected is copied.

To move the copied file in a folder which you created, double-click the folder for it to open. Then right-click inside the opened folder and select **Paste** icon indicated in the photo below.

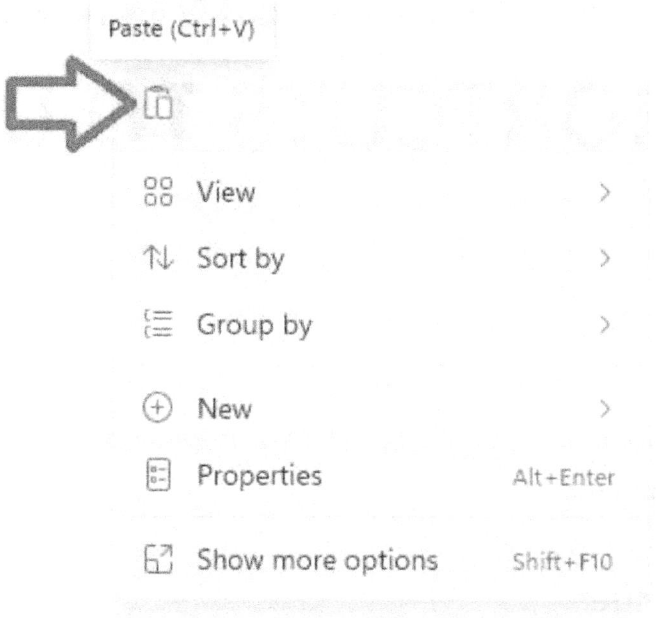

Immediately you click the **Paste icon**, the file is moved into the folder.

You can also use a shortcut to paste the copied file into the folder. To do so, double-click the folder to open it. Then, on the computer keyboard, press the Ctrl and V keys to paste the copied file into the folder.

Dragging Files Around in a Folder

Another method for moving files on your computer is by dragging them. For years, PC users have found this to be the quickest way to move files.

To move files to a folder, first select the files. You can select multiple files on the same line at the same time. To do so, move your cursor to the first file you want to start the selection from, then press the left mouse button and move in one direction to select the other files.

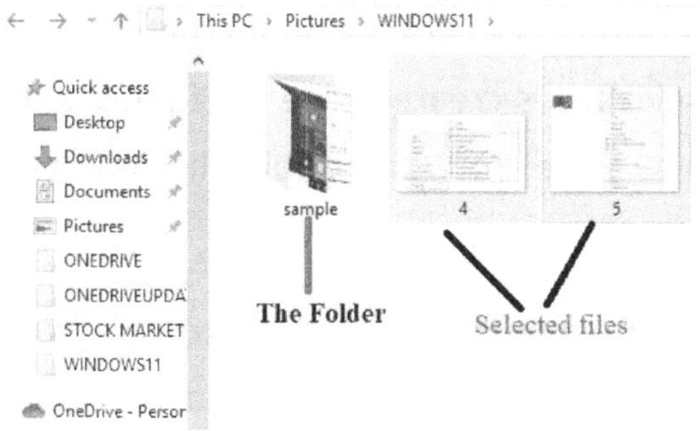

Remove your finger from the left mouse. Press down the left mouse again and drag the select files over the folder you want to move the files. Remove your finger from the left mouse. At this point, you have succeeded in moving the files to a folder.

How to Create Zip Files and Folders in Windows 11

Zip files can be created on a PC running Windows 11. By the way, what exactly are Zip files? Zip files are collections of files that have been compressed and placed in a folder. Zip files are compressed so that they are smaller than their actual sizes.

The purpose of compressing files in a Zip folder is to make the contents less bulky and thus faster to transfer. If you want to get my ebooks on Microsoft Word, Excel, PowerPoint, Publisher, and Access, I can have them in Zip format before sending them to you. This makes the files lighter and easier to transfer.

To create a Zip file from a folder on my computer that contains many other files, I must first right-click on the folder. This action will generate numerous options.

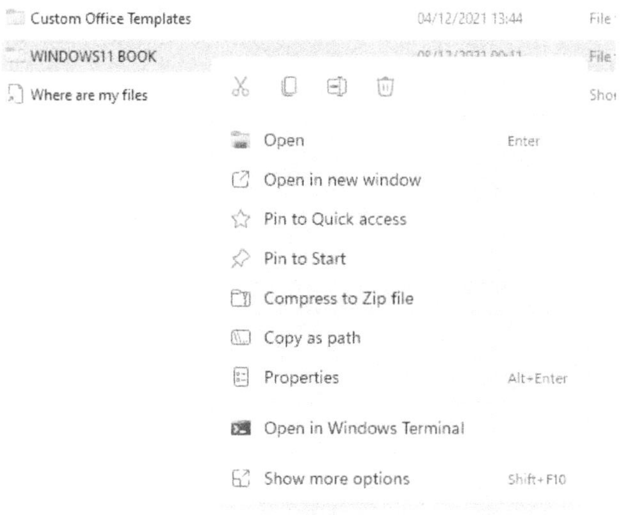

Out of those options you see, click **Compress to Zip file**. Immediately you give that command, the Zip files of that folder you previously selected is created. The Zip folder contains the same files but just that they are compressed in their new state. You can double-click on the Zip folder to access the files that are contained in it.

As an additional knowledge, when someone sends a Zip file to you, you need to extract those files before you start accessing them. To extract those files contained in the Zip folder, right-click the folder and select the option **Extract All**.

And lastly, click **Extract** button. Once the extraction process is completed, you can then start accessing the individual files easily.

CHAPTER 12

HOW TO SETUP AND USE THE WINDOWS SUITE PRODUCTIVITY TOOLS - WORD, EXCEL & POWERPOINT

Setting up Microsoft Office 365

For you to set up Office 365, you have to install it.

Access your Microsoft Account.

Go to your account's home page and select 'Install Office.' Depending on your account category, the page will appear.

When you've finished downloading, go to 'Finder' and select 'Downloads.'

Double-click on Microsoft Office.

When the installation screen appears, tap 'continue' to begin.

Examine and then accept the software license agreement.

Choose how you want the installation to be done (either with particular apps or the entire suite).

Check the disk requirements and the installation location, then click 'Install Software.' After this, your Office 365 should be ready.

Using the Office Apps

Launch an Office application such as Word, Excel, or PowerPoint.

Enter your Microsoft account password and email address.

Choose 'Accept' on the 'Accept the license agreement' screen.

The office application will launch, and you will be able to create spreadsheets and office documents.

CHAPTER 13

SECURITY SETTINGS, ANTIVIRUS AND WINDOWS DEFENDER

Lock, Disconnect Or Shut Down

When we say "lock" your PC, we don't mean a physical key (or even a keyhole-style lock like the one found on PCs in the 80s and 90s). Instead, we'll go over how to use the software locking feature that comes standard with Windows.

During a power outage, Windows shows you how to log back in, but your Windows session is still running in the background. You can return to your previous activity at any time by logging into your account on the login screen with your password, PIN, or other methods of login.

"Log out" prevents other people from using your computer, without erasing everything you've worked on Windows. It also shuts down everything and turns off the computer completely.

Using a Keyboard Shortcut to Lock

The quickest way to lock Windows 11 is to press Windows + L. If you press Windows + L at any time, Windows will freeze and you will be able to log in immediately.

To lock, use the Start menu.

To quickly lock your computer, click the Start button, then your username, and then "lock" from the menu that appears. Lock can also be selected from the Start menu.

By clicking the Start button, then choosing your account name from the drop-down menu in the lower-left corner, you'll be able to start the process. In the menu that comes up, choose "lock." If your computer doesn't work, you'll have to sign back in to use it again until it does.

Ctrl + Alt + Delete will lock your computer.

To quickly lock your PC, use Ctrl + Alt + Del on the desktop. To access it, simultaneously press the Ctrl, Alt, and Del keys on your keyboard. A black screen will appear with a menu in the center. To lock your computer, simply press the "Lock" button.

Auto-locking via dynamic lock

Check the box in Settings that says "Allow Windows to automatically lock your device when you're not around."

A third option, Dynamic Lock, allows you to lock your computer when you leave it. To begin, connect your smartphone to your computer via Bluetooth. Then, connect your smartphone to your computer. Press Windows+i to access Settings. Then, navigate to Accounts > Sign-in options to learn how to sign in. Maintain an eye on "Dynamic lock." While you're in that area, make sure the box next to "Allow Windows to automatically lock your device when you're not there" is checked. After that, you can click Install. The next time you leave your computer, Windows will recognize that you have moved and will lock it for you.

The screen goes to sleep as soon as the person stops doing anything.

Choose the screensaver you want to use in the "Screen saver settings" window and select "When resetting, show the login screen."

Windows 11 also locks itself after a certain amount of time. This also works if you frequently leave your computer in a shared space with other people. To do so, open Start and type "screensaver" into the search box. Choose "Settings" from the results, and then "Turn screen saver on or off" from the drop-down menu.

When the "Screen saver settings" window appears, select a screensaver from the drop-down menu. Then, in the "Wait" box, enter a time to tell your computer how long you want it to wait before it locks. When you're finished, check the box next to "Show the log-in screen when you reboot." Then click "OK." The next time the computer is left unused, a screen saver is activated, and the computer locks itself.

If you don't like how it looks, you can change it in Settings> Personalization> Lock Screen if you don't.

Enable Or Disable Windows Security In Windows 11

To access Windows Security, click the Start button and then select Settings from the menu that appears. Another way to access the Settings menu quickly is to use the Windows Key + I keyboard shortcut.

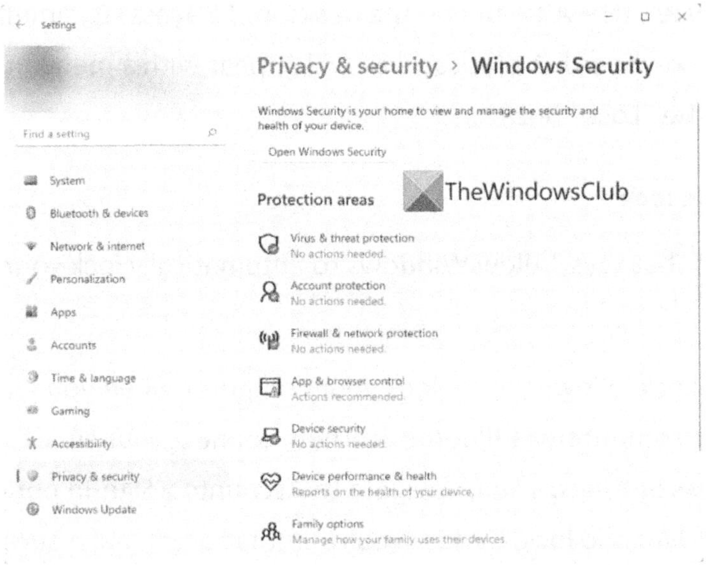

- Configuration is open.
- When the Settings box appears, from the drop-down menu, select Privacy and Security> Windows Security.
- Finally, click the Open Windows Security option to confirm your selection.
- Launch Windows Security.

This will launch the Windows Security application. Different safeguards are provided by the department and the state.

Security Risk

- Left-click to disable Virus & Threat Protection (your built-in antivirus protection). Click the Manage settings link in the "Antivirus settings and threats" section.
- Enable and deactivate the desired protection. Real-time protection is an essential component of Windows security: if you turn it off, you will receive a notification to turn it back on. • If you turn it off, it will turn off for a limited time but will automatically turn back on. This is useful if your anti-virus program is preventing you from accessing a file that you know is safe.

Using Group Policy, Disable Microsoft Antivirus

If you're running Windows 11, you can disable anti-virus software permanently by using Group Policy. You must first disable "Spoofing Protection" in the Windows Security app before proceeding.

Tamper protection guards against unauthorized system changes. If you tampered with the security and made changes to the Group Policy, Windows Security will undo the changes the next time you restart your computer.

Disable Tamper Protection

To disable spoofing prevention, press the Start button (or the Windows keys) and type Windows Security: Choose Best-suited from the drop-down menu on the top right.

Then, select Virus and Threat Protection>Manage Settings. Scroll down and turn off the Tamper Protection setting.

Tamper protection is disabled.

You can continue to modify Group Policy in order to permanently disable Windows Security Antivirus.

Using Group Policy Editor, permanently disable Windows Defender Antivirus

To use the Group Policy Editor to disable Windows Security Antivirus, press the Start or Windows keys. Then enter gpedit and choose the best match.

When the Local Group Policy Editor appears after you launch the program, go to the following path:

Microsoft Defender Antivirus> Computer Configuration> Administrative Models> Windows Components>

Then, on the right side of the screen, double-click the policy labeled Disable Microsoft Defender Antivirus.

To disable antivirus, select Enabled, then click Apply and OK.

For the change to take effect, you must restart Windows 11. When you open Windows Security, you will notice that virus and threat protection is disabled.

You don't have to go back to Group Policy to turn it back on. Instead, in the Windows Security app, click the Allow button.

When you restart, keep in mind that Windows Security antivirus will be turned off. Nonetheless, the "Shield" icon will remain on the taskbar. This is because the icon is part of the overall Windows security application, not just the anti-virus program.

Other parts of the security suite will continue to function as long as real-time anti-virus is disabled. For example, you can open Windows Security and enable or disable additional safeguards such as Defender Firewall.

Windows 11 Privacy Preferences

Now that you're up to speed on the significance of data privacy, let's look at the various privacy settings in Windows 11.

Options for general security

Each Windows user has a unique advertising ID associated with their specific device; if enabled, this advertising ID allows companies to use the data collected for their own purposes. By disabling the Windows Advertising ID, you can prevent the app from displaying personalized and targeted advertising.

The steps to configure the standard security settings in Windows 11 are as follows:

Select Privacy and security> General to open the General section of the Settings menu.

Set Allow apps to show me personalized ads using the My Advertising ID button to enable or disable advertising ID settings.

Similarly, by accessing the list of languages, you can choose whether websites can show you relevant content and whether Windows can follow the launch of applications to improve the Start menu.

CHAPTER 14

MUST-HAVE APPS TO INTERACT WITH OTHERS AND HOW TO SET THEM UP

The Windows 11 Mail App

Email has come a long way from its humble beginnings, and there are many ways for you to access your mail using apps or your web browser. Use the Mail app or other email clients to send and receive messages instantly.

Setting Up a New Email Account

Using the Start menu, launch the Mail app.

If this is your first time using the app, choose Add account.

If you have previously used the app, go to Settings at the bottom of the navigation pane on the left, then select Manage Accounts.

Select the type of account you want to create. You have the option of using an existing Outlook account or creating a new one. You can also use an account from Office 365, Google, Yahoo, or iCloud. You can also use POP or IMAP email accounts, but this will necessitate more advanced configuration options.

If you select a Google account and have enabled two-step verification (recommended), you will be prompted to enter your unique 2-step verification code, which will be sent to your email or phone number.

Enter the required sign-in information, including your email address and password.

When you click Done, your account will begin syncing. The mail app will automatically download all of your emails and contacts.

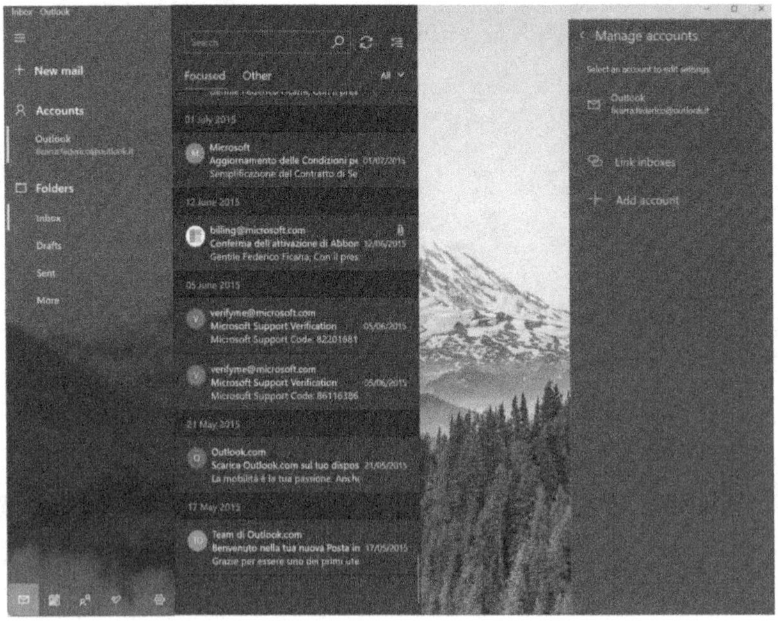

Using the Mail App

In the navigation pane on the left side of the Mail App, you will see several buttons.

- Collapse - collapses the navigation pane to reduce clutter.
- + New mail - compose a new email.
- Accounts - View your account information.
- Folders - includes your Inbox, Drafts, Sent, and Archive folders.
- Switch to Mail - Used to toggle between the Mail and Calendar apps.
- Switch to Calendar - used to toggle between the Mail and Calendar apps.
- Settings - access the Mail App settings.

You will see a search bar, a refresh button, and a selection mode button in the messaging list pane. You can use the search bar to look for specific terms or keywords in your emails. The refresh button will initiate a download and upload of all incoming and outgoing mails. The selection mode can select specific emails for deletion or move them into a different folder. Finally, the reading/writing pane is on the right side of the window.

How to Compose an Email

In the navigation pane, click the + New Mail button.

On the right side of the window, a new writing pane will appear.

In the 'To:' field, enter your recipient's email address.

You can send an email to multiple people at the same time by entering their email addresses here. The other email addresses you've included will be visible to your recipients.

You can also add people to your email's CC list. Because CC stands for "carbon copy," you can use this feature to send a copy of the email to someone who is not the primary recipient. When sending work emails, the CC feature comes in handy: you can send something to a colleague and CC your manager to keep track of all communications.

In the Subject line, type a title for your email.

Fill in the text field with your email address.

Many options are available at the top of the writing pane, including Format, Insert, Draw, and Options.

Text formatting tools such as Bold, Italics, Underline, Bullet lists, and Styles are available in Format.

Insert lets you add files, tables, images, or links to your email.

With the Draw tools, you can add freehand notes or doodles to your emails. Text can also be highlighted or circled.

The Options tab includes spell checking tools, zoom and find tools, and the ability to mark your emails as high or low priority.

When you've finished writing your email, press the Send button.

You can delete anything in your email by clicking the Delete button.

How to Listen to Music or Watch Videos

There are several ways you can listen to music on your Windows 11 computer. You can use streaming services like Spotify or use a media player to listen to CDs or mp3s already on your computer.

Music Streaming

Spotify

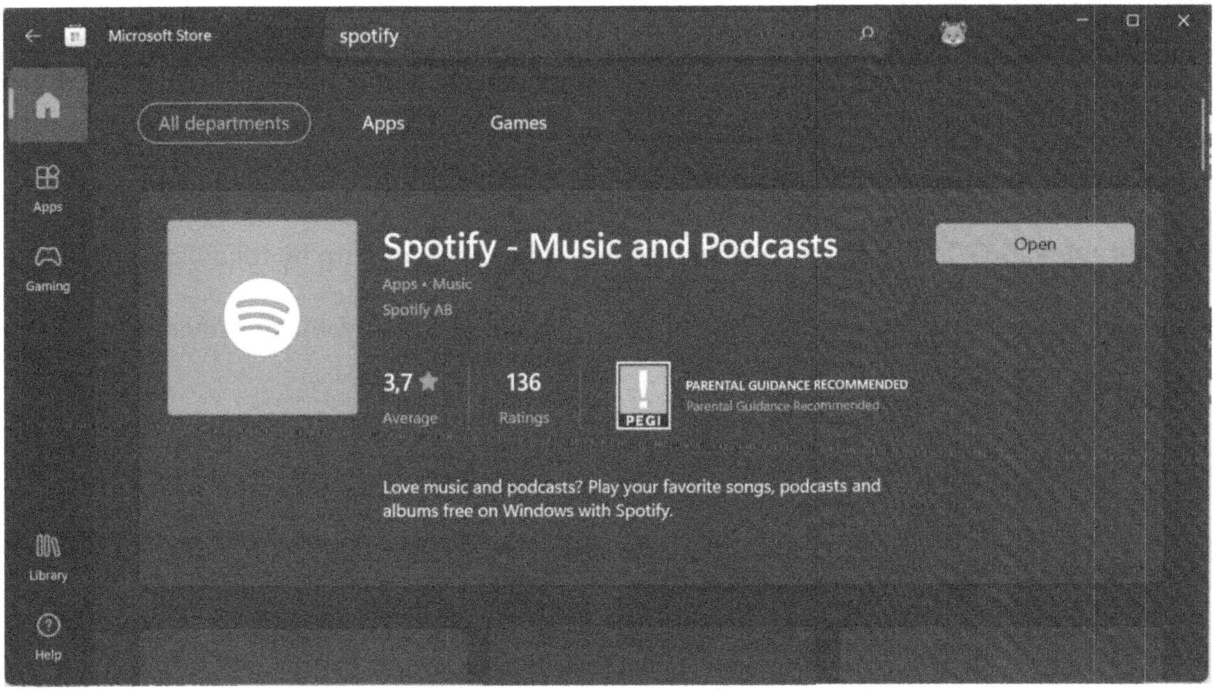

The Spotify app is available for download from the Microsoft Store.

After installing the app, launch it and sign in with your existing password and email address, or create a new account.

You can use multiple devices to sign into the same Spotify account, allowing you to take your music and playlists with you wherever you go.

Use the buttons on the left side to navigate the Spotify app:

Search for new songs, artists, and genres to listen to.

Allow Spotify to create a custom playlist based on a song, album, playlist, or artist you've chosen.

Your Music - locate your most recently played songs, songs, albums, artists, and radio stations that you enjoy. You can also find Local files, which contain downloaded content for offline listening.

Playlists - Here you can find your favorite playlists as well as Spotify's playlists with new music.

You can browse and discover new music or listen to your favorites in the app's middle section. To find specific tracks, artists, or albums, use the search bar at the top.

To pause, skip, adjust volume, and shuffle settings, use the player at the bottom of the app.

Add friends to see what they're listening to on the right side of the app. You can also send your music to friends.

Spotify Premium

The free version of Spotify gives you access to the entire music and podcast library, but you may be interrupted by advertisements on a regular basis. The free version also prevents you from downloading content to listen to it later.

To fully utilize the app's features, you must subscribe to Spotify Premium by following these steps:

Log in to Spotify using your email address/username and password at www.Spotify.com.

In the menu bar, select 'Upgrade.'

Choose the type of membership and price point you want to pay for.

Enter your payment information, then refresh your desktop app to gain access to Spotify Premium.

Windows Media Player and Groove Music

Both of these apps are included with Windows 11 and can play the majority of media files. They allow you to listen to music and create playlists. You can find either app by searching for it in the Start menu.

The main difference is that Groove Music can be installed on multiple devices and will sync your songs, artists, albums, and playlists across these devices so you can listen to your music wherever you go.

VLC Media

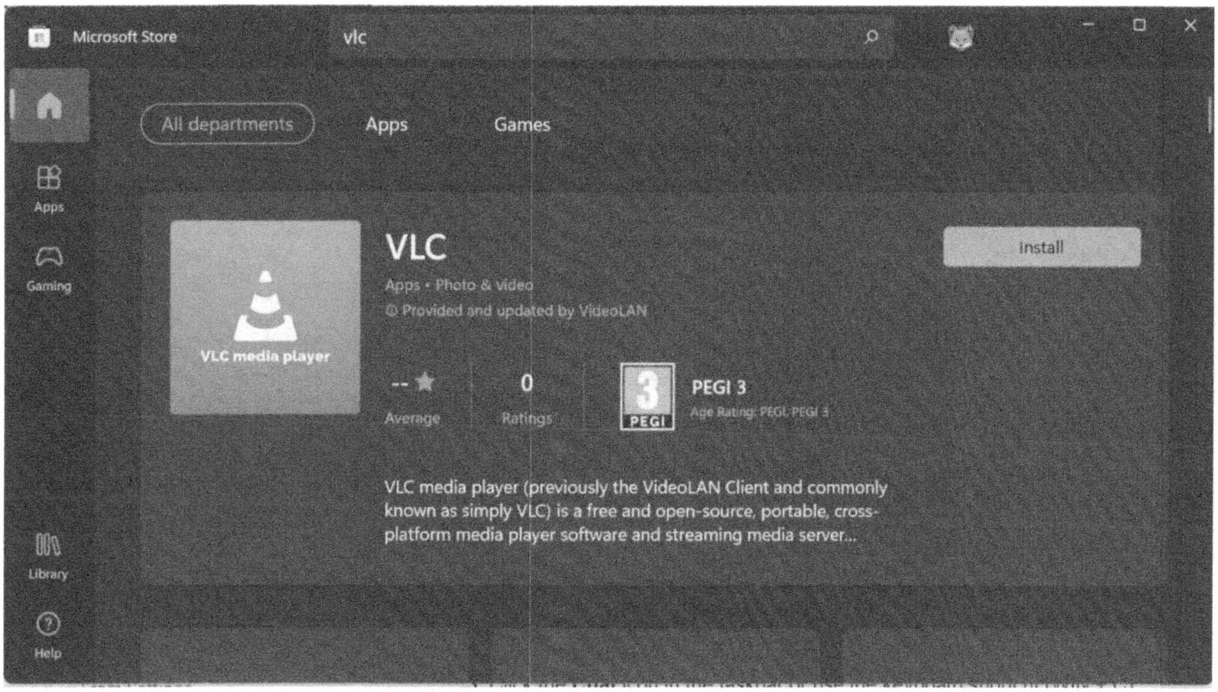

VLC is a third-party media player that can be used to view or listen to almost any kind of media file, including videos, music, podcasts, and more. It is a very simple to use and easy-to-understand app.

To load media into VLC, find the content in File Explorer and drag it directly into the open VLC app window.

CHAPTER 15

BEST TIPS AND TRICKS

Keyboard and Touchscreen Shortcuts in Windows 11

Although it has always been possible to place two different windows side by side on the desktop, Windows 11 has expanded on this concept by allowing you to place more than two windows side by side. When all of your windows are visible on the desktop, copying and pasting information between them becomes much easier. When you drag a window to a corner, Windows 11 provides an onscreen grid that helps you position all of your open windows.

Another notable feature of Windows 11 is the enhancement of virtual desktops, which allows for the creation of multiple separate desktops. Windows and programs for one project can be aligned on one desktop while you switch to a second desktop to place windows for another project.

There are new commands for manipulating actions onscreen and these benefit touchscreen owners. They are described below;

Snapping Windows

TO DO THIS	PRESS THESE KEYS
Snap window to the upper-right corner	Windows key + →, and then Windows key + ↑
Snap window to the upper-left corner	Windows key + ←, and then Windows key + ↑
Snap window to the lower-right corner	Windows key + →, and then Windows key + ↓
Snap window to the lower-left corner	Windows key + ←, and then Windows key + ↓

Touchscreen controls

TO DO THIS	PRESS THIS
Open the Widgets panel	**Slide a finger inwardly from the left edge**
To view the current month's calendar and the Notifications panel	**Slide a finger inwardly from the right edge**
Keep all open apps minimized in the taskbar to reveal the desktop	**Slide three fingers down the screen**
To place your minimized windows back	**Slide three fingers back up the screen**
To switch quickly between apps that are open	**Slide three fingers to either the left or right**
To switch between any virtual desktop that is open	**Slide four fingers to either the left or the right**

However, if your laptop doesn't include a touchscreen rather a trackpad, most of these gestures would still perform well on your laptop.

Windows 11 Touch Commands

Windows 11 works flawlessly on touchscreens, whether built into tablets, laptops, or even desktop monitors in the absence of desktop monitors. When using a touchscreen device, the commands listed below will help you navigate Windows 11.

Press and hold: Doing so will reveal detailed information without requiring you to act. When you press and hold, a menu with more options usually appears.

The mouse equivalent is: If you move your cursor over an item, the details of that item will be displayed; if that doesn't work, right-click on your mouse.

When you tap on something, an action is performed; for example, an app is launched, a link is followed, or a command is executed.

The mouse equivalent is: Simply click the mouse to perform an action.

Drag items across a tablet's screen as easily as you would a piece of paper across a tabletop. The slide action is typically used to scroll through pages or a list, but it can also be used for other interactions such as moving an object, drawing, or even writing.

The mouse equivalent is: You use a mouse to click, hold, and drag the item. A scroll bar appears frequently near the edge of the screen, allowing you to change your view simply by dragging the box in the scroll bar.

Pinch or stretch: This is as simple as pinching or stretching a piece of paper. Simply placing two fingers on the screen and moving them accordingly produces an expanded or shrunk result, depending on the action performed.

Keyboard and mouse equivalent: Locate the control key on the keyboard and press it while using the mouse wheel to zoom or minimize the item on the screen.

Turn by rotating two fingers on the screen in the same way you would move a piece of paper on your desktop. The object onscreen would move in sync with your finger movements. Hold Mouse has no equivalent.

CHAPTER 16

MAINTENANCE, BATTERY, UPDATES AND DIAGNOSTIC

View Your Battery Settings

If you are using a mobile device such as a laptop, tablet, or smartphone, Windows 11 allows you to view the power usage of your battery. A graph of your battery levels over time can be found in Settings > Power & battery. You can also see a list of battery usage by app. Use this feature to quickly identify and change the settings of apps that are consuming too much power. You can change some settings, such as limiting background processes to only run when the app window is open.

Keeping Windows 11 Up-to-Date

Microsoft stated that with Windows 11, there would be fewer major updates to manage. There should be only one major update per year, but there will almost certainly be much more frequent smaller updates, either to non-essential software or security updates. Many critical updates will be installed automatically, without your intervention, but some larger updates may necessitate your participation.

Stay Up-To-Date

Keeping the operating system up to date is important, and should be one of the first steps you take to making your PC more secure.

1 - To check for updates awaiting installation, open Settings > Windows Update. If nothing is shown, click the "Check for updates" button.

2 - Any updates discovered will be shown at the top of the screen. The update will be titled in a way that makes it clear what it is for, such as "Cumulative Update for Windows 11" or "Security Update for Windows Defender."

3 - Click the "Download & Install" button to begin adding an update. The status will be displayed to the right of the update. While you wait, you can do other things on your computer. The installation will not be hampered if the window is closed.

4 - A system restart is almost always required to complete the update process, so go back into Windows Update to double-check. When you're finished installing the update, click "Restart now."

5 - If you don't want to restart right away (perhaps because you're in the middle of something else), you can schedule it for a later time.

Pausing Updates

As mentioned, essential security (and other) updates will download and install in the background, without needing action from the user. If, for whatever reason, you want to stop automatic updates, you can use the Pause Updates feature.

1 - Open Settings > Windows Update. Under the More Options section you will see the Pause Updates option. The default option is "Pause for 1 week".

2 - To apply the pause, click this, or use the dropdown menu to select a longer pause period. When you press the pause button, the text changes to "Extend for 1 week." To extend the pause, click the button.

3 - To resume updates earlier than the schedule you selected, simply click the "Resume updates" button at the top of the Windows Update section.

Uninstall any installed updates.

If you notice something wrong with your computer after installing an update, you should uninstall it to see if that was the source of the strange behavior.

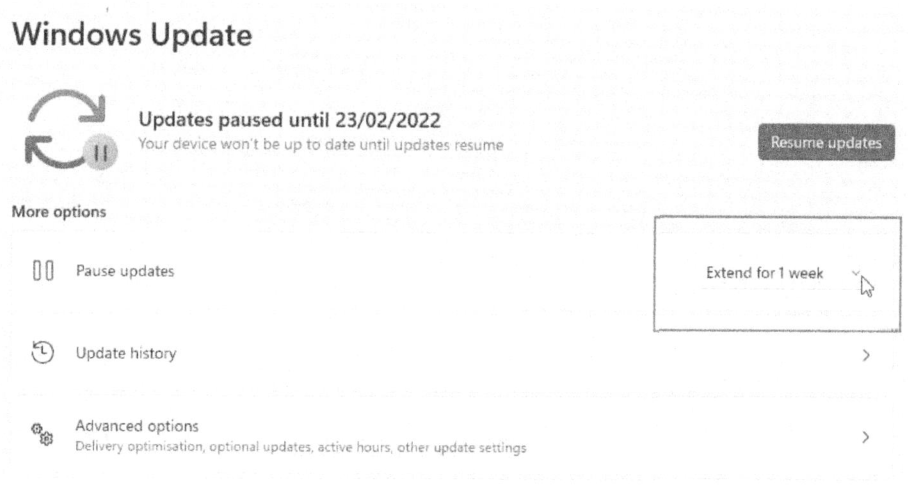

First, navigate to Settings > Windows Update > Update History. Scroll down to the bottom of the screen and select "Uninstall Updates."

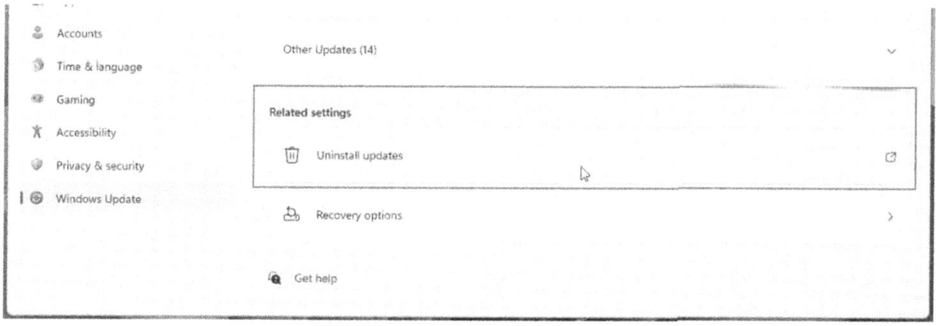

In the new window that opens, find the update that you suspect of causing the problem in the list of installed updates. Select the update and then click "Uninstall", or right-click it and "Uninstall".

Restart your PC and check that the problem is no longer appearing.

CHAPTER 17

FAQS

Why can I not change the color of my taskbar?

Normally, you would not be able to change the color of your taskbar when using the 'Light Mode' feature. You must first change the default mode to dark mode. After that, choose an accent color for both the Start and Taskbar. The color of both bars is changed automatically as a result of this process. You could also use themes, which would change the color automatically.

Why did the color of my toolbar suddenly change?

Follow the steps below to resolve this issue.

- Select 'Settings.'
- Select 'Personalization.'
- Select 'Accent Color.'
- Select any color you want by tapping the 'Manual' icon.

As a result, the color that appears on your toolbar remains fixed as the color you select.

How do I change the color of the font on my toolbar to black?

You cannot change the color of your fonts immediately, but you can check the preview by following the steps below.

- Select 'Settings' • Select 'Personalization'
- Select 'Colors.'
- Select 'Custom colors'.
- Select 'View Colors.'

Will the indexing feature cause my computer to slow down?

The search indexing feature makes your computer search faster and more efficiently. You get to look through several files at once and get a clear answer. The only time the feature appears to slow down the operation of your computer is when you are using a computer with low specifications. As a result, your computer's CPU suffers and it begins to run less efficiently. When you notice this, try turning off the Search Indexing feature.

CONCLUSION

Thank you for reading this book. Windows 11 includes a slew of new features to help users with productivity, creativity, and gaming. It enables you to connect with people you care about more quickly and access the best apps via the newly designed Microsoft Store.

This guide has covered everything there is to know about the latest operating system, such as navigating through the File Explorer, managing settings, creating a local or Microsoft account, projecting to a wireless display, booting into safe mode, how desktop works, and much more.

You should now be able to download, install, and use Windows 11 on your PC after reading this guide. Please leave an honest review so that others can buy it to solve their Windows 11 problems.

Good luck!

Made in United States
North Haven, CT
10 November 2026

22088884R00050